Fatima 2017

Paul De Marco

Copyright 2016

Paul De Marco

ISBN : 978-1-326-60659-6

2

-Contents-

Introduction

Introduction

In the spring of 1915 Europe was embroiled in the horror of the First World War and the ferocious battle of Gallipoli had just begun. Unlike in previous wars innocent civilians found themselves as targets too and a shocking example of this was the sinking of the cruise liner Lusitania twelve miles off the Irish coast on 7th May of that year, which claimed 1198 lives. However the tiny village of Aljustrel in the parish of Fatima in Portugal was largely untouched by the war and the town had absolutely no claim to fame at that time. But events in this sleepy farming village over the next two years were about to rock the Catholic Church and have a profound effect on World history.

Three young children claimed that they'd seen a vision of the Virgin Mary on the **13th of May 1917** at a place named the Cova da Iria and they said that she had asked them to return there on the 13th of each month over the next six months. During this period the children were given various secrets as well as a terrifying **vision of Hell**, but the secrets were only made public many years later.

Our Lady said that World War I would soon end, but she warned that unless mankind repented and turned from sin, that a more devastating war would break out during the pontificate of Pius XI. She called for the pope in conjunction with the bishops of the World, to consecrate Russia to her and Our Lady also asked for a devotion to be made to her, in reparation for the sins against her Immaculate Heart. She promised to be present with the graces necessary for salvation, at the time of death of all those who made this First Five Saturdays devotion.

Our Lady gave an assurance that if these requests were met, that the World would enjoy peace and that Russia would be converted. If not, then mankind would again experience war and Russia would spread her errors throughout the World. She said that the sign that the World was about to be chastised for its sins would be a night illumined by an unknown light.

The disbelieving villagers and priests made life difficult for Lucia and her cousins, Francisco and Jacinta and even their own parents thought that they were lying. However the visions continued and the children said that Our Lady would give a sign on the 13th of October 1917, so that all would believe. A massive crowd estimated at 70,000 descended on the Cova da Iria that day and stood in the mud and the driving rain.

Simple farmers; journalists; scientists, believers and non-believers alike, were left stunned by what they saw - the **Miracle of the Sun**.

However despite this astonishing miracle, mankind and also the Church were very slow to respond and there was indeed a night illumined by an unknown light on the **25th of January 1938**, which was visible throughout Europe. Just six weeks later Germany annexed Austria and the World was on the road to a war which would claim 85 million lives and our history books show us the effect that Russian imperialism subsequently had on the World.

Francisco died in 1919 aged ten and Jacinta died at the age of just eight the following year, both victims of the Spanish Flu outbreak, which killed at least 3% of the global population. Lucia survived and would play a pivotal role in sharing the message of Fatima with the World throughout her life. She committed the text of the third secret to writing on the 9th of January 1944 and placed it in a sealed envelope, which was ultimately taken to the Vatican thirteen years later on the 16th of April 1957. Here it lay unopened in a little chest in the office of Pope Pius XII. Pope John XXIII and Pope Paul VI both read the secret, but would not make it public for whatever reason.

On **13th May 1981**, the anniversary date of the first apparition in 1917, there was an assassination attempt on John Paul II as he was being driven slowly through the crowds in St Peter's Square. The Pope was totally convinced that Our Lady had saved his life and so he requested all the documentation on the appearances at Fatima. Ultimately the pope did consecrate Russia to the Immaculate Heart of Mary on the 25th of March 1984. Since then, the World has witnessed the collapse of the Soviet Union, which began with the dismantling of the Berlin wall on 9th November 1989. The bullet which so nearly took the Pope's life is now set in the crown of the statue of Our Lady of Fatima!

Eventually the text of the third secret and an interpretation of it were made public on the **26th of June 2000**, some 83 years after Lucia had witnessed the vision and this caused massive controversy.

This book gives a fascinating account of the story of Fatima from the very first apparitions of an angel in 1915 through to the present day, set in the context of World history. It looks at the response of the Church and at the timeless message that Our Lady gave the children, which is every bit as relevant today as it was back in 1917.

-Chapter 1-
An angel prepares the way

Lucia dos Santos was born to her parents Antonio and Maria Rosa on the 22nd of March 1907 and she was the youngest of seven children. The family had some plots of arable land on which they farmed vegetables and they also owned a small flock of sheep. One of her older sisters helped earn money for the family by working as a weaver and the other as a seamstress, both working from home.

The residents of Aljustrel were mainly farmers and the town is located about 75 kilometres south of Coimbra and 120 kilometres north of Lisbon and still only had a population of below 10,000 in 2011.

Lucia was baptised when she was only eight days old and her mother ensured that she, along with her other children, were raised in the Catholic faith. Maria was happy to let some of the other mothers bring their young children to her house so that they could go off to work and so Lucia was always surrounded with other youngsters. They were happy days and she was particularly fond of her cousins, Francisco and Jacinta Marto, who lived just two houses away.

Francisco was about 14 months younger than Lucia and Jacinta was three years younger than her, but the cousins had very different personalities, with Jacinta being outgoing and effervescent whereas Francisco was quiet, calm and submissive in nature. They would play their favourite games together using buttons or little pebbles as forfeits, with Jacinta typically winning Lucia's buttons, which meant that she had to remove them from her clothes and risk a scolding from her mother. Fortunately her sisters were usually around to stitch them back on before her mum found out.

The village often held dances and festivals and Lucia and Jacinta both loved to dance whereas Francisco preferred to play his flute and observe the proceedings from a distance. At Carnival time everyone would be involved in preparing food for the banquet, in making costumes and dancing and the festivities would go on well into the night for three whole days.

Maria gave catechism lessons to her own children but often the cousins were there listening to her as well as the neighbour's children. It was customary for the children to first receive Holy Communion at the age of ten and only after the parish priest was satisfied that the child had a reasonable understanding of their faith. Maria's lessons paid dividends and the young Lucia was allowed her first Communion at the age of just six.

At the age of seven Lucia was given responsibility for taking the sheep out to find pasture on the slopes of the hillsides nearby. Her sister Carolina had been doing this but she was now twelve years old and her mother felt that it was time that she found work for herself. Lucia soon befriended three other young children who were looking after their families flocks and so she spent her days in their company. They were Maria Rosa and her sister Teresa Matias and Maria Justino.

Lucia was unsure of the exact date but it was certainly in 1915 when she witnessed the first apparition. In her memoirs which she wrote many years later, she described it happening between the months of April and October 1915 and she based this on how she remembered the weather having been at the time.

She and her friends had led their flocks high up on a hill which was known as the Cabeco and from this vantage point on the southern slope they had a beautiful view of the tree covered valley below them.

At around midday they ate their pack lunches and were just about to start to pray the Rosary together, something that was customary to do in Portugal in 1915. It was then that Lucia and her friends witnessed a vision of an illuminated figure of human form, but without any distinctive features, that was suspended above tree level. She described the figure as resembling a statue made of snow, yet appearing to be virtually transparent. They were mesmerised by this apparition and watched it until it finally disappeared from their sight.

Lucia said that it looked like a person wrapped up in a sheet and she would be teased mercilessly for this later, even by her own sisters. Lucia's three companions rushed back to tell their families and although Lucia had decided to keep quiet about what she'd seen, it soon got back to her mother. Maria Rosa was distinctly unimpressed on hearing this rumour and simply said, "childish nonsense!"

However these four children witnessed the same apparition on two further occasions on the very same hillside and Lucia kept the incidents to herself. Again the apparition seemed to have no discernible features, nor did it speak to them. After these events her friends again told their families about what they'd seen and news was soon reported back to Maria, who then took it upon herself to scold poor Lucia.

Jacinta couldn't wait for her older cousin Lucia to return each day and as soon as she heard the tinkling noise of the bells on the sheep, she would come running over to meet her. Shortly after this third encounter, Francisco and Jacinta were allowed to start taking their own sheep out to pasture and so Lucia opted to leave her three girl friends and spend her time with the cousins instead.

There was some land in the foothills of the eastern slope of the Cabeco that Lucia's family owned, called Chousa Velha and one day in the spring of 1916 the trio led their flocks to pasture there. It began to drizzle and so they walked higher up on the hillside to take shelter under an overhanging boulder which was in an olive grove. After their snack lunch they said the customary Rosary, but instead of saying the full prayers they abbreviated them to just saying 'Our Father' and 'Hail Mary' on the beads, so that they could quickly get back to their games.

By now the rain had stopped, the air was calm and the sun was shining brightly, but from nowhere a strong wind came up which shook the trees and made them all look up. There above the olive trees they saw the apparition coming towards them, which Francisco and Jacinta had not previously witnessed. Although Lucia hadn't spoken to them about the vision, it's likely that they would have heard of the prior sightings from the other children in the village.

The children were dumbstruck with amazement at the sight of this apparition, which Lucia described as having been dazzlingly white and transparent like crystal, with strong sunlight shining behind it. As it came closer they could discern its features better and they could see that it had the appearance of a young man, around the age of fourteen or fifteen.

The apparition said, "Do not be afraid! I am the Angel of Peace. Pray with me." The angel bowed down until his head actually touched the ground and asked them to repeat a prayer, which he recited with them three times over:

"My God, I believe, I adore, I hope and I love you! I ask pardon of You for those who do not believe, do not adore, do not hope, and do not love You." The angel also said, "Pray thus. The Hearts of Jesus and Mary are attentive to the voice of your supplications."

The angel disappeared but the three children remained on their knees repeating this prayer over and over again. The spiritual experience was so intense and all-encompassing that the children couldn't even speak to each other. The 'spiritual atmosphere' as Lucia described it, was still felt by the children the next day and only gradually faded away.

Lucia and Jacinta could both hear what the angel had said, but Francisco could only see the angel and hear what Lucia was saying. Understandably the shock of this apparition and the words of the angel had a profound effect on them and they spent a lot of their time in the fields, kneeling in prayer and repeating the words given them over and over again.

Later that year, during the summer of 1916, Lucia and her cousins Jacinta and Francisco again saw the angel, but this time it was while they were playing by a well at the bottom of the garden belonging to her parents. During the summer the children would bring the sheep back from the hillside before midday so as to avoid the heat and they would find shade under the trees by this well.

The angel said, "What are you doing? Pray, pray very much! The most holy Hearts of Jesus and Mary have designs of mercy on you. Make of everything you can a sacrifice, and offer it to God as an act of reparation for the sins by which he is offended, and in supplication for the conversion of sinners. You will thus draw down peace upon your country. I am its Angel Guardian, the Angel of Portugal. Above all, accept and bear with submission the suffering which the Lord will send you."

This is how Lucia described the words of the angel:

'They were like a light which made us understand who God is, how He loves us and desires to be loved, the value of sacrifice, how pleasing it is to Him and how, on account of it, He grants the grace of conversion to sinners.'

Once again Francisco was unable to hear the angel speak but he could hear what Lucia was saying during the apparition. At Cabeco the angel had announced himself as the Angel of Peace, but it's uncertain whether this angel and the Angel of Portugal were one and the same, as Lucia herself believed to be the case. The children somehow managed to keep these apparitions to themselves perhaps to avoid being ridiculed by the children and some adults in the village.

After this appearance Jacinta said, "I don't know how I feel. I can no longer talk, or sing, or play. I haven't strength enough for anything."

Francisco replied, "Neither have I. But what of it? The angel is more beautiful than all of this. Let's think about him."

A few months later in late September or early October they were again at the Cabeco at their hide-out under the overhanging rock, with their heads to the ground saying the prayer that the angel had previously given them. Suddenly they were immersed in a wonderful, supernatural light and raising their heads they saw the angel in front of them.

He held a chalice in his left hand and above the chalice, suspended in mid air, was a host and drops of blood fell from the host into the chalice. The angel let the chalice go, which was then left suspended in the air with the host above it, and knelt down with the children to pray.

He asked them to recite this prayer three times:

"Most Holy Trinity, Father, Son and Holy Spirit, I adore You profoundly and offer You the most precious Body, Blood, Soul and Divinity of Jesus Christ, present in all the tabernacles of the world, in reparation for the outrages, sacrileges and indifference with which He Himself is offended. And, through the infinite merits of His most Sacred Heart, and the Immaculate Heart of Mary, I beg of You the conversion of poor sinners."

After Lucia and her cousins had recited this prayer three times, the angel stood up and took the Host in one hand and the Chalice in the other. He placed the Host on Lucia's tongue and then gave the blood from the chalice to Jacinta and Francisco.

The angel said, "Eat and drink the Body and Blood of Jesus Christ, horribly outraged by ungrateful men! Make reparation for their crimes and console your God."

The angel then prostrated himself on the ground and repeated the prayer he had taught them another three times with the children. The angel vanished but the children remained for several hours with their heads to the ground reciting the new prayer.

In her memoirs Lucia said: 'the force of the presence of God was so intense that it absorbed us and almost completely annihilated us. It seemed to deprive us even of the use of our bodily senses for a considerable length of time.'

For several days after this apparition Francisco felt unable to speak but he later said, "I love to see the Angel, but the worst of it is that, afterwards, we are unable to do anything. I couldn't even walk. I don't know what was the matter with me."

He also said to Lucia: "The Angel gave you Holy Communion, but what was it that he gave to Jacinta and me?"

It was Jacinta who answered: "It was Holy Communion, too. Didn't you see that it was the Blood that fell from the Host?"

He replied, "I felt that God was within me, but I did not know how!"

The angel's prayer is similar to the one that Jesus gave to Sister Maria Faustina of the Sisters of Our Lady of Mercy, when he appeared to her in her convent at Vilnius on 13th and 14th September 1935:

'Eternal Father, I offer You the Body and Blood, Soul and Divinity of Your dearly beloved Son, our Lord Jesus Christ, in atonement for our sins and those of the whole world.'

There's more detail about Sister Faustina and the Chaplet of Divine Mercy prayers in chapter 14, which covers the subject of Hell.

This was the sixth and last time the angel appeared to Lucia, but now visitations by the angel would give way to visitations by the Virgin Mary herself.

-Chapter 2-
Our Lady appears to the children

By this time Lucia's mother had sent all her daughters out to work and so the house was much quieter than usual. In fact during the day it was only Lucia, her brother and her mother who were at home until her father arrived back from work. Lucia was still looking after the sheep and her brother was taking care of the vegetables and olive trees on the small plots of land the family owned. As with most mothers, Maria didn't adjust too well to the sudden quiet in the house and frequently burst into tears as she missed her other daughter's company so much.

This in turn resulted in Lucia getting upset and so she would often go down to the well to cry it all out. Jacinta and Francisco would sometimes meet her there and it seems that one of the remarkable qualities of Jacinta was that she had so much empathy. She would be there with her arm around Lucia comforting her and she would often say, "My God, it is as an act of reparation, and for the conversion of sinners, that we offer You all these sufferings and sacrifices."

Jacinta would give her lunch to the poor children she encountered on the way to pasture the sheep and in many other little ways kept true to the request of the angel that she should offer her trials and difficulties up as a sacrifice to God. Lucia recalled that her mother became seriously ill about the time of the first apparition of Our Lady to the children in May 1917.

First appearance of Our Lady: 13th May 1917

On the morning of Sunday 13th May 1917, Lucia and her cousins led their sheep to an area just north of Aljustrel for them to pasture and this land belonged to Lucia's father and was called Cova da Iria or peaceful hollow. The 13th of May is a significant date in the Church as it is the feast of Our Lady of the Blessed Sacrament.

This was a time of tremendous destruction and fear in Europe as World War 1 had been raging for almost three years. By this time there had been the carnage of the battles at Mons; Ypres; Gallipoli; Loos, Verdun and the Somme. Lloyd George had become Prime Minister of

Great Britain on 7th December 1916 and America had finally also declared war on Germany on 6th April 1917, a full two years and eight months after Britain had.

However in the fields around Cova da Iria about two kilometers from Aljustrel there was complete tranquility as Lucia, her cousins and a few dozen sheep arrived. As the sheep grazed, the children climbed higher up the hillside and were playing together when they saw a brilliant flash of light. Although the sky was cloudless they thought that it could have been lightning and so they decided to take the sheep home and out of harms way. They had moved the flock about half way down the slope when they suddenly saw a second bright flash of light in the sky.

It was then that they witnessed an apparition of a dazzlingly bright lady dressed completely in white. She appeared to be standing on top of a small Holm oak (Holly oak) sapling which was about a metre high. As with the vision of the angel, she radiated an intensely brilliant light, far brighter than that of the sun. Lucia described her as follows:

"She was more brilliant than the sun and radiated a light clearer and more intense than a crystal glass filled with sparkling water, when the rays of the burning sun shine through it."

The children were astounded at this apparition which was only a few feet in front of them and they were immersed in the brilliant light which radiated from her. The ten year old Lucia was unafraid of this vision and later recalled that she had felt peace, joy and happiness in her presence. In some ways this was the same emotion she had felt in the presence of the angel, but on those occasions the children had felt an urge to fall to the ground and they found it difficult to move and even to talk. In the presence of the lady Lucia felt great exultation and she also felt relaxed in speaking to her.

The lady simply said, "Do not be afraid. I will do you no harm."

Lucia innocently asked her, "Where are you from?" to which the lady replied, "I am from heaven."

Lucia then said, "What do you want of me?"

To this the lady replied, "I have come to ask you to come here for six months in succession, on the 13th day, at this same hour. Later on I will tell you who I am and what I want. Afterwards I will return here yet a seventh time."

Lucia then asked, "Shall I go to Heaven too?"

She replied, "Yes, you will."

Then Lucia said, "And Jacinta?" to which the lady replied, "She will go also."

Finally she asked, "And Francisco?" to which she replied, "He will go there too, but he must say many Rosaries."

Lucia then plucked up the courage to ask about two other people she knew of, who had recently died. The one was Maria who had died at about the age of sixteen and the other was Amelia who had died when she was about eighteen to twenty years old. These girls frequently used to visit her house to be taught how to weave by her eldest sister.

Lucia asked, "Is Maria das Neves in Heaven?" and the lady replied, "Yes, she is."

Then she said, "And Amelia?" to which the lady said, "She will be in purgatory until the end of the world."

Her reference to purgatory is highly significant, as this subject is virtually never covered by priests in their homilies today and it's as though purgatory has been quietly dropped from the teachings of the Church and this will be discussed later in the book.

The Lady then asked the children, "Are you willing to offer yourselves to God and bear all the sufferings He wills to send you, as an act of reparation for the sins by which He is offended, and of supplication for the conversion of sinners?"

To this they bravely replied, "Yes, we are willing!"

The lady then said, "Then you are going to have much to suffer but the grace of God will be your comfort."

Lucia said that as the lady spoke these words she opened her hands and transmitted an intense, penetrating light from them and it seems that it was through this light that she communicated with the children in a special way. Lucia described it as follows:

"Our Lady opened her hands for the first time, communicating to us a light so intense that, as it streamed from her hands, its rays penetrated our hearts and the innermost depths of our souls, making us see ourselves in God, Who was that light, more clearly than we see ourselves in the best of mirrors. Then, moved by an interior impulse that was also communicated to us, we fell on our knees, repeating in our hearts, 'O most Holy Trinity, I adore You! My God, my God, I love you in the most Blessed Sacrament!'"

Before she departed Our Lady said, "Pray the Rosary every day, in order to obtain peace for the world, and the end of the war."

Her statement here clearly shows that prayer can affect the events unfolding in our World and that outcomes are not indelibly written into the future history of mankind!

After saying this, the children saw Our Lady slowly rise up into the air in an easterly direction, with a light surrounding her and that also preceded the direction of her movement, until she finally disappeared from view.

Again all three children saw the apparition of Our lady, but Francisco was unable to hear what she had actually said. When Lucia told him that she had said that he would go to Heaven, he was overjoyed and said, "Oh my dear Our Lady! I'll say as many rosaries as you want!"

He was very diligent in praying the rosary from then on and would often be in prayer while Lucia and Jacinta played together. Lucia recalled him saying one day: "I loved seeing the Angel, but I loved still more seeing Our Lady. What I loved most of all was to see Our Lord in that light from Our Lady which penetrated our hearts. I love God so much! But He is very sad because of so many sins! We must never commit any sins again."

After this visitation by Our Lady, Jacinta was unable to keep the experience to herself and told her parents what had happened. Lucia and Francisco had both wanted to keep the matter a secret, at that stage anyway, in order to avoid undue attention in the village.

However news spread very quickly throughout the town of Jacinta's claim to have seen Our Lady and this caused problems for the children as their parents again thought they'd made the whole story up. As more people heard of the apparition it put increasing pressure on Maria to get Lucia to admit that she had lied about the vision and even Lucia's sisters joined in the verbal abuse.

Second appearance: 13th June 1917

This was the feast date of Saint Anthony, the patron saint of Portugal and was widely celebrated throughout the country at that time. The villagers would dress up for the occasion and hold a dance afterwards. However this year instead of joining their families in the public celebrations, the three children planned to return to the Cova da Iria as arranged, in the hope of seeing Our Lady again.

Lucia took the sheep out to pasture at daybreak and had intended to bring them home in time for her to attend mass at 10am. However her brother ran out to tell Lucia to come home straight away as several men and women from the surrounding villages had arrived outside their house and wanted to see her. These people asked if they could accompany Lucia to the Cova da Iria that morning, perhaps out of curiosity, to which Lucia agreed, but she first attended the 8 am mass.

The sight of strangers waiting outside the house further infuriated Maria, who became even more determined to get Lucia to admit that she'd been lying all along. It was a very difficult time for Lucia and she was frequently found in tears by Jacinta who would try to console her. She would say, "Don't cry. Surely, these are the sacrifices which the Angel said that God was going to send us. That's why you are suffering, so that you can make reparation to Him and convert sinners."

When they arrived at the Cova the children began praying the Rosary and by now there were a few dozen people from the surrounding villages who had accompanied them. As soon as they'd finished praying the Rosary they saw bright flashes of light approaching and then Lucia, Francisco and Jacinta saw Our Lady standing on top of the oak sapling nearby, just as she had done the previous month.

It had been a whole month since the children had first seen the Blessed Virgin and so they clearly had enough time to plan what they would say should they see her again.

Lucia asked, "What do you want of me?"

Our Lady answered, "I wish you to come here on the 13th of next month, to pray the rosary every day, and to learn to read. Later I will tell you what I want."

Lucia then mentioned someone who was ill and asked if he could be healed, to which Our Lady replied, "If he is converted he will be cured during the year."

Lucia then said, "I would like to ask you to take us to heaven."

Our Lady answered, "Yes. I will take Jacinta and Francisco soon. But you are to stay here some time longer. Jesus wishes to make use of you to make me known and loved. **He wants to establish in the world devotion to my Immaculate Heart. I promise salvation to those who embrace it, and those souls will be loved by God like flowers placed by me to adorn his throne."**

This beautiful promise by Our Lady refers to the devotion of the first five Saturdays which she would outline in detail to Lucia later.

Lucia then asked, "Am I to stay here alone?" to which the lady replied, No my daughter. Are you suffering a great deal? Don't lose heart. I will never forsake you. My Immaculate Heart will be your refuge and the way that will lead you to God."

After this Our Lady opened her hands from which intensely bright and penetrating rays emerged to immerse the children in. Lucia noted that Jacinta and Francisco were in the part of light which rose towards Heaven but that she was in a section of light that shown down towards the Earth. They said that it felt as though they were immersed in God's love.

Lucia also described seeing something else in this encounter:

"In front of the palm of Our Lady's right hand was a Heart encircled by thorns which pierced it. We understood that this was the Immaculate Heart of Mary, outraged by the sins of humanity, and seeking reparation."

Again Francisco was unable to hear Our Lady speak and he asked Lucia, "Why did Our Lady have a Heart in her hand, spreading out over the world that great light which is God? You were with Our Lady in the light which went down towards the earth, and Jacinta was with me in the light which rose towards heaven!"

Lucia replied, "That is because you and Jacinta will soon go to heaven while I, with the Immaculate Heart of Mary, will remain for some time longer on earth." Francisco said, "How many years longer will you stay here?" to which Lucia replied, "I don't know. Quite a lot."

Francisco then asked, "Was it Our Lady who said so?" and Lucia replied, "Yes, and I saw it in the light that shone into our hearts."

This last statement shows that Our Lady was indeed communicating with the children through the rays of light emanating from her and not through verbal communication alone.

Francisco, referring to the onlookers then said, "These people are so happy just because you told them that Our Lady wants the Rosary said, and that you are to learn to read! How would they feel if they only knew what she showed to us in God, in her Immaculate Heart, in that great light! But this is a secret. It must not be spoken about. It is better that no one should know it." These were remarkably mature words for a boy who had just celebrated his 9th birthday two days earlier!

Many of the residents of Aljustrel believed that Lucia and her cousins had simply imagined the encounters. However some accused them of outright lying and so Maria Rosa and her brother Ti, father of Jacinta and Francisco, took the three children to the local parish priest, Father Ferreira. After questioning the children the parish priest came to the conclusion that it made no sense for Our Lady to make an appearance in order to ask the people to pray the rosary each day, as most people did this anyway. He also noted that the children were unwilling to divulge all the information that they claimed they had been given. He observed that in instances where divine revelations had been made in the past that the person receiving them would have to divulge everything. He then suggested that if they had indeed experienced something supernatural then it could have been of satanic origin!

These comments by their local priest were devastating for Lucia and her cousins and caused them a great deal of anguish. Lucia's response was to seek solitude and she would wander off to be alone, even avoiding Jacinta and Francisco. As she dwelled on the comments made by the priest, she eventually resolved not to go back to the Cova on the 13th of July. Francisco pleaded with her on a few occasions to change her mind and even stayed awake the whole night praying to Our Lady for Lucia to have a change of heart. It must have worked, because on that morning she felt an irresistible pull to go back to the Cova again.

Third appearance and the vision of Hell: 13th July 1917

By now word of the apparitions had spread and so on Friday 13th July there were about four thousand people lining the streets waiting to accompany the children in the hope of seeing Our Lady. When they reached the Cova da Iria the crowds began praying, with many of them saying the rosary out loud together. As Lucia, Francisco and Jacinta approached the sapling oak, there were flashes of bright light and Our Lady once again appeared above the tree.

Lucia boldly asked, "What do you want of me?"

Our Lady replied, "I want you to come here on the 13th of next month, to continue to pray the Rosary every day, in honour of Our Lady of the Rosary, in order to obtain peace for the world and the end of the war, because only she can help you."

Lucia, clearly upset by the locals and her parish priest disbelieving her, then asked, "I would like to ask you to tell us who you are, and to work a miracle so that everybody will believe that you are appearing to us."

Our Lady replied, "Continue to come here every month. **In October I will tell you who I am and what I want, and I will perform a miracle for all to see and believe.**"

The young Bernadette at Lourdes was treated in a very similar way to Lucia and the disbelief of the villagers is reminiscent of the crowds that refused to believe in the divinity of Jesus, unless he constantly worked miracles in front of their eyes. Jesus himself stated that his miracles should be seen as evidence that he was God's son. John 10:36:

"Why then do you accuse me of blasphemy because I said, 'I am God's son'? Do not believe me unless I do what my Father does. But if I do it, even though you do not believe me, believe the evidence of the miracles that you may know and understand that the Father is in me, and I in the Father."

Lucia also asked for the healing of several people and Our Lady replied by saying that the sick must pray the rosary in order to obtain the grace of healing during that year. She also added, "Sacrifice yourself for sinners, and say many times, especially when you make some sacrifice: 'O Jesus, it is for love of You, for the conversion of sinners, and in reparation for sins committed against the Immaculate Heart of Mary.'"

After saying this she opened her hands to reveal the intense light in which the children were once again immersed but on this occasion they were then given a terrifying vision of Hell. This vision of Hell would remain a secret until Lucia finally wrote it down on 31st August 1941. It was after this that the Vatican subsequently published 'The message and secret of Fatima' on **13th May 1942**.

"The rays of light seemed to penetrate the earth, and we saw, as it were a sea of fire. Plunged in this fire were demons and souls in human form, like transparent burning embers, all blackened or burnished bronze, floating about in the conflagration, now raised into the air by the flames that issued from within themselves together with great clouds of smoke, now falling back on every side like sparks in huge fires, without weight or equilibrium, amid shrieks and groans of pain and despair, which horrified us and made us tremble with fear. The demons could be distinguished by their terrifying and repellent likeness to frightful and unknown animals, black and transparent like burning coals. Terrified and as if to plead for succour, we looked up at Our Lady, who said to us, so kindly and so sadly:

'You have seen hell where the souls of poor sinners go. To save them, God wishes to establish in the world devotion to my Immaculate Heart. If what I say to you is done, many souls will be saved and there will be peace. The war is going to end; but if people do not cease offending God, a worse one will break out during the pontificate of Pius XI. When you see a **night illumined by an unknown light**, know that this is the great sign given you by God that He is about to punish the world for its crimes, by means of war, famine and persecutions of the Church and of the Holy Father. To prevent this, I shall come to ask for the **consecration of Russia to my Immaculate Heart**, and the **Communion of Reparation on the First Saturdays**. If my requests are heeded, Russia will be converted, and there will be peace; if not, she will spread her errors throughout the world, causing wars and persecutions of the Church. The good will be martyred, the Holy Father will have much to suffer, various nations will be annihilated. In the end, my Immaculate Heart will triumph. The Holy Father will consecrate Russia to me, and she will be converted, and a period of peace will be granted to the world. In Portugal, the dogma of the faith will always be preserved ..'"

After saying this, Lucy, Francisco and Jacinta were given another vision, which came to be known as the **third secret of Fatima**. After this vision had been revealed to the children Our Lady said, "Do not tell this to anybody. Francisco, yes, you may tell him."

She also said: "When you pray the Rosary, say, after each mystery: 'O my Jesus, forgive us, save us from the fires of hell. Lead all souls to heaven, especially those who are most in need."

Finally Lucia asked, "Is there anything more that you want of me?" Our Lady replied, "No, I do not want any more of you today." Then, as after the other appearances Our Lady rose in an easterly direction and soon disappeared from their view.

Lucia later wrote what Francisco had said of the rays of light that they had been immersed in: "We were on fire with that light which is God, and yet we were not burnt! What is God? We could never put it into words. Yes, that is something indeed which we could never express! But what a pity it is that He is so sad! If only I could console him!"

The 'fire' that the children saw, which in some ways resembles the appearance of physical fire, but does not combust material immersed in it, is reminiscent of what Moses witnessed with the burning bush.

Exodus 3:2: There the angel of the Lord appeared to him in flames of fire from within a bush. Moses saw that though the bush was on fire it did not burn up.

The vision of Hell left a lasting impression on the children especially Jacinta, who was filled with horror at what she'd seen. After seeing this vision any penance or sacrifice she made even if it caused her suffering, was as nothing if it could only help prevent souls from going to Hell.

Lucia recalled in her third memoir that Jacinta would often sit on the ground and say, "Oh Hell! Hell! How sorry I am for the souls who go to Hell! And the people down there, burning alive, like wood in the fire!" She would then kneel down for long periods of time reciting the prayer that Our Lady had given the children: "O my Jesus! Forgive us, save us from the fire of Hell. Lead all souls to Heaven, especially those who are most in need."

After this vision Jacinta regularly intervened if she heard children or even adults within earshot speaking crudely or saying anything unkind and she would tell them plainly that they were offending God. It was as though she put aside any concern for her own embarrassment or popularity so as to ensure that they steered away from sin.

Lucia also recalls her saying, "Francisco! Francisco! Are you praying with me? We must pray very much, to save souls from Hell! So many go there! So many!"

And on another occasion she asked Lucia, "Why doesn't Our Lady show Hell to sinners? If they saw it, they would not sin, so as to avoid going there! You must tell Our Lady to show Hell to all the people. You'll see how they will be converted."

Sometimes Jacinta would pick wild flowers and sing a hymn she made up herself, "Sweet Heart of Mary, be my salvation! Immaculate Heart of Mary, convert sinners, save souls from Hell!"

So the first secret revealed to the children was the vision of Hell. The second was a request for the consecration of Russia to the Immaculate Heart of Mary and the establishment of a devotion to her through the communion of reparation on the first five Saturdays.

However on 13th July 1917 Our Lady said that the children should keep these revelations secret i.e. a secret at that time. She gave no specifics about the communion of reparation devotion to her and she also said that she would return later to ask for the consecration of Russia to Her Immaculate Heart.

The children therefore did as they'd been instructed and kept quiet about these revelations. It was only on **10th December 1925** that Our Lady appeared to Lucia with the child Jesus in her room at the Dorothean convent near Pontevedra in Spain and gave specific details of the **First Five Saturday's devotion**.

On **15th February 1926** the child Jesus again appeared to her, this time in the convent gardens, and again asked for this devotion to Our Lady and Lucia then revealed this request to her confessor and also to the Mother Superior of the convent.

Our Lady appeared to Lucia on **13th June 1929** when she was at the Dorothean Novitiate near Tuy, to ask for the **consecration of Russia to Her Immaculate Heart** and Lucia then wrote an account of this revelation for her confessor, Father Goncalves. More detail on these three appearances to Lucia are given later in the book.

The secret of the vision of Hell was only revealed in her third memoir which she finished writing on **31st August 1941** while she was at Tuy.

The third secret revealed to the children caused enormous speculation and controversy for decades to come. Initially the speculation centred on why the Church had not released Lucia's description of the prophetic vision at all. Later after its eventual release, the controversy was around whether or not the entire transcript had been made public or not.

It's quite incredible that the Vatican only made the contents of this letter i.e. the third secret, known on **26th June 2000** about 83 years after the vision had first been given to Lucia and this is also covered later in the book.

Even after the 13th July apparition, Maria Rosa was still convinced that Lucia was lying and she again dragged her off to the parish priest to get her to admit to this. However after being questioned by the priest in great detail about what she'd seen, Lucia still refused to recant.

The mayor of the town of Ourem, which had jurisdiction over Fatima, was a young man named Artur de Oliveira Santos. He sent a message to Jacinta and Francisco Marto's home and to Lucia's parents to say that he wanted to interview all three of the children in Ourem, which was nine miles away. Lucia's uncle said that he wouldn't allow Francisco and Jacinta to go as they were far too young, but Lucia's parents were happy for her to go there and answer the questions.

So early the next day, Lucia accompanied by her father and her uncle, set off for Ourem with Lucia riding on a donkey, which she fell off three times along the way. At the administration office attempts were made to force Lucia to reveal what she'd seen and heard and to promise never to return to the Cova da Iria again. Artur de Oliveira Santos made all manner of threats against Lucia, but she refused to talk and in the end she was released and allowed to go home.

This is similar to what happened to Bernadette at Lourdes, where after the 6th apparition on 21st February 1858 she was taken to the Police Commissioner's house to be interrogated. However an angry crowd gathered outside his house and Bernadette was released. She was again interrogated after the 9th apparition by the town's Imperial Prosecutor and later by a magistrate after the 11th apparition. As with Lucia, the young Bernadette had to face her local priests who were disbelieving of her accounts. It was only after the 16th apparition on 25th March 1858, when Bernadette repeated to Father Peyramale the words of Our Lady, **"I am the Immaculate Conception"** that he finally believed her. This doctrine of the Church had only been recognised four years earlier and it would have been impossible for Bernadette to have made this up. Fittingly the 25th of March is the Feast of the Annunciation.

The crowds that had descended on the Cova meant that Lucia's family couldn't grow vegetables any more, as the whole area had been churned up by the feet of thousands of visitors. Lucia's mother was distraught but still couldn't get her daughter to admit to lying, despite her verbal threats and occasional beatings with a broom handle!

Lucia was later questioned in minute detail by the Reverend Dr Formigao, but despite the thoroughness of his examination she would not reveal the secrets nor contradict herself. Lucia actually became very fond of him and he then came on a regular basis to interview her on the events at the Cova da Iria.

On Monday 13th August 1917 great crowds had gathered in the village in the hope that they might see Our Lady. However the children were unable to walk to the Cova that day due to another intervention by Artur de Oliviera Santos and what he did would be unthinkable in our modern World.

He sent a message to Lucia's home instructing her to go immediately to her aunt's house and so Antonio walked with his daughter the short distance over to the Marto's home, which was difficult in itself due to the massive crowds that had gathered there.

Many villagers wanted to ask the children what Our Lady had said and others were asking for the children to petition her to cure their relatives of various illnesses. In the house they found Artur already there and he quickly set about interrogating the children in order to extricate the secret they'd been given, but he was again unsuccessful.

He then took the children to the house of the Parish priest, Father Ferreira, but after a short while he put them in his horse drawn carriage and drove them off to Ourem, apparently without their parent's knowledge or consent. When word reached the crowds that the children had been taken to Ourem, instead of being allowed to go to the Cova, there was a near riot. In Ourem the children were questioned yet again about what had happened at the Cova but they still refused to talk.

Later that day and after various threats were made against them, they were thrown into a communal cell which was the public jail of the town. They were told that they had to wait there, while a cauldron of oil was boiled and that if they did not confide their secrets then they would be executed in it.

It beggars belief that children could be treated in this way and poor Jacinta, who was born on 11th March 1910, was only seven years old at the time. Even the other prisoners in the cell tried to get the children to talk, either to save them from harm, or perhaps to help get themselves released. Jacinta, believing that she was about to die, then took a religious medal from her pocket and asked one of the prisoners to put it on a nail in the wall for her.

She knelt down to pray the rosary with Lucia and Francisco and incredibly the other prisoners knelt down to pray with them. Considering that he was in prison and believing that he was under threat of imminent execution, Francisco was also extremely brave. However he was highly distressed that they would be unable to meet Our Lady at the Cova as she had asked them to do.

He said, "Our Lady must have been very sad because we didn't go to the Cova da Iria, and she won't appear to us again. I would so love to see her!"

After a few hours they were removed from the cell and locked in another room, believing that they were about to be executed. Still they refused to talk and so Jacinta was taken out first and led away. Some time later Francisco was led away, thus leaving poor Lucia all alone.

The door was unlocked again and then Lucia was led away, but to her immense relief it was not to be executed, but to another room where her cousins were waiting for her. Artur kept them in Ourem for another night, but realising that they weren't going to talk, he took them back to Fatima in his carriage and left them outside the presbytery of the church, not even bothering to take the traumatised children home.

Fourth appearance: 19th August 1917

On the Sunday following their release from custody in Ourem, Lucia, Francisco and his older brother Joao were tending their sheep at Valinhos which is near Aljustrel. Joao Marto had been with Lucia when the angel appeared to her for the second time in 1915, although he'd been unable to see the apparition himself.

Prior to seeing anything unusual at all, the three children could feel something supernatural approaching them. Lucia wanted Jacinta to be present and so she asked Joao to run back to the house and fetch her. At about 4pm there was a flash of bright light as had preceded all the other appearances. Our Lady then appeared over a Holm oak sapling and Lucia again asked, "What do you want of me?"

Our Lady replied, "I want you to continue going to the Cova da Iria on the 13th and to continue praying the Rosary every day. **In the last month, I will perform a miracle so that all may believe.**"

Lucia asked, "What do you want done with the money the people leave in the Cova da Iria?"

She answered, "Have two litters made. One is to be carried by you and Jacinta and two other girls dressed in white; the other one is to be carried by Francisco and three other boys. The money from the litters is for the festa of Our Lady of the Rosary, and what is left over will help towards the construction of a chapel that is to be built here."

Lucia said, "I would like to ask you to cure some sick persons" to which Our Lady replied, "Yes, I will cure some of them during the year."

Lucia said that Our Lady looked very sad as she said, "Pray, pray very much, and make sacrifices for sinners; for many souls go to hell, because there are none to sacrifice themselves and to pray for them."

Unlike at the other appearances, Our Lady did not immerse the children in the light from her hands, but simply rose up and disappeared from view in an easterly direction. After this visit the children thought up all manner of ways to offer little sacrifices to God, including wearing a rope tied tightly around their waists which caused them a lot of discomfort. They would often go without food or drink and would give their lunches to the poor children they encountered along the way.

It's important to note that only the children could see Our Lady at these apparitions, but the crowds couldn't see her at all, although they sometimes saw the phenomena associated with her presence. Francisco was overjoyed that Our Lady had returned again as he'd been having doubts since his imprisonment in Ourem that she would do so.

Many of the visitors to the Cova da Iria came on mules and the land had been so trodden underfoot that it was now useless for growing their vegetables or to provide pasture for their sheep. Maria Rosa reluctantly had to sell the flock with the exception of three sheep as they were so in need of money.

Lucia was constantly being sought by a never-ending stream of people asking to speak to her about what she'd seen, what Our Lady had said and to give her various petitions. In addition to this she was continually being called to give an account of herself to various outside priests as well as to the parish priest. Unfortunately many of the villagers still thought the children were lying and on some occasions Lucia was given a slap or a kick in addition to the verbal abuse she was being given.

Fifth Appearance: 13th September 1917

A massive crowd of about thirty thousand started making their way to the Cova da Iria in anticipation of another apparition. The crowds were pressing against the children, with some of them falling on their knees begging them to petition Our Lady for a miraculous cure or some other request. As they moved along someone even reached out and cut off Lucia's plaits of hair, but she was unperturbed by this. People were even climbing the trees and standing on top of walls along the road from Aljustrel to Fatima and they shouted down to the children as they walked by. Lucia said that the chaotic scene reminded her of the Gospel accounts in which Our Lord was surrounded by thousands of people as he walked along.

When they reached the Holm oak at the Cova da Iria the majority knelt down in prayer, saying the rosary and many were calling out for the healing of their family members who were ill. The children also began to pray the Rosary and again there was a bright flash of light and soon afterwards our Lady was there with them, standing above the tree.

She said, "Continue to pray the Rosary in order to obtain the end of the war. In October Our Lord will come, as well as Our Lady of Dolours and Our Lady of Carmel. Saint Joseph will appear with the Child Jesus to bless the world. God is pleased with your sacrifices. He does not want you to sleep with the rope on, but only to wear it during the day time."

Lucia said, "I was told to ask you many things, the cure of some sick people, of a deaf mute ..."

She replied, "Yes, I will cure some, but not others. **In October I will perform a miracle so that all may believe.**"

Again there were no rays emanating from Our Lady's hands on this appearance but Francisco was overjoyed when Lucia told him that Jesus would appear with Our Lady at the next visit.

Although the spectators couldn't see the Virgin Mary, two other supernatural events were observed by thousands in the crowd that day. Shortly before the appearance of Our Lady, the sky darkened at around midday and a luminous globe or 'ball of fire' as some described it, was seen moving through the sky. Most described it as being oval and not perfectly round.

Padre Joao Quaresma who witnessed the phenomenon described it as follows:

"To my great astonishment I saw, clearly and distinctly, a luminous globe coming from the east and moving to the west, gliding slowly and majestically through space. With my hand I motioned to Monsignor Gois who was standing next to me, and who had been making fun of me for coming. Looking up he too saw this unexpected vision. Then suddenly this globe, giving off an extraordinary light, disappeared from my sight, and Monsignor Gois, also, saw it no longer."

The second phenomenon occurred as Our Lady departed and her departure was accompanied by the falling to Earth of white 'petals' accompanied by a supernatural light. These were described as looking like round, shining snowflakes. The phenomenon was also unusual in that the luminescent objects became smaller as they got closer to Earth, instead of appearing bigger, before vanishing without a trace.

-Chapter 3-

The Miracle of the Sun

Not everyone was convinced that these visions were real and there were even rumours circulating that the authorities had planned to detonate a bomb close to the site of the apparitions, to dissuade people from gathering there. However the events that would unfold this day would shatter any illusion that the children had been lying. Like the doubting Thomas, who on touching the risen Jesus standing right in front of him, could only utter the words, 'My Lord and my God.'

Sixth appearance: Saturday 13th October 1917

Lucia, Jacinta and Francisco left home early on the morning of Saturday 13th October as they thought it likely that they would be delayed by the crowds along the way. Heavy rain was falling and there were massive crowds lining the roads. Lucia's parents were concerned for her safety and decided to go with her to the Cova for the first time and so her father walked along, holding Lucia's hand.

It's thought that about 70,000 people arrived on the hillside in great anticipation of seeing a miracle on this day, although some estimates put the number as high as 100,000. Either way, it was a massive crowd that gathered in the torrential rain which soon turned the Cova into a field of mud. Lucia asked the crowds to close their umbrellas and to pray the Rosary and despite the conditions, the crowds went down on their knees in the mud to pray.

Then a distinctive blue coloured column of smoke was seen rising to a height of about two to three metres above the heads of the children. This smoke column, which dissipated after a minute or so, had been witnessed on the previous five visits by Our Lady as well. By now the tree at the site of the apparitions had been stripped of its foliage by people wanting to take a leaf or two home with them as a souvenir. The townsfolk had however built an arch at the site and so Lucia, Jacinta and Francisco went there instead. Lucia then asked the crowds to start reciting the Rosary again, which they did.

After the lightning flash that always preceded her appearances, Our Lady appeared in their midst, again above the ground. Lucia then asked her innocent prayer of faith, "What do you want of me?"

Our Lady answered, "I want to tell you that a chapel is to be built here in my honour. I am the Lady of the Rosary. Continue always to pray the Rosary every day. The war is going to end, and the soldiers will soon return to their homes."

Lucia then said, "I have many things to ask you: the cure of some sick persons, the conversion of sinners, and other things…"

Our Lady replied, "Some yes, but not others. They must amend their lives and ask forgiveness for their sins."

She went on, "Do not offend the Lord our God any more, because He is already so much offended."

Lucia wrote that Our Lady looked very sad when she said these words.

After this Our Lady then opened her hands and projected her own light onto the sun as she ascended into the sky and Lucia said that she felt an interior impulse to call out, 'Look at the sun.'

She wrote: "After Our Lady had disappeared into the immense distance of the firmament, we beheld St Joseph with the child Jesus and Our Lady robed in white with a blue mantle, beside the sun. St Joseph and the Child Jesus appeared to bless the world, for they traced the Sign of the Cross with their hands. When, a little later, this Apparition disappeared, I saw Our Lord and Our Lady; it seemed to me that it was Our Lady of Dolours. Our Lord appeared to bless the world in the same manner as St Joseph had done. This apparition also vanished, and I saw Our Lady once more, this time resembling Our Lady of Carmel."

There are many eyewitness accounts of the breathtaking solar phenomenon that tens of thousands of people witnessed that day. Terrified onlookers describe having seen the sun dance or spin in the sky and at one point appear to almost fall to the Earth, before returning to its normal size and position. The event was witnessed not just by the massive crowd at the Cova, but by people up to eighteen kilometres away.

Despite this, no observatories recorded anything unusual that day, further indicating that it was a relatively localised miraculous event. It's also interesting that not everyone in the crowd saw the phenomenon and this is reminiscent of the Gospel accounts when the voice of God was heard speaking to Jesus and some in the crowd disbelieved.

John 12:27: "Now my heart is troubled, and what shall I say? 'Father, save me from this hour'? No, it was for this very reason I came to this hour. Father, glorify your name!" Then a voice came from heaven, "I have glorified it, and will glorify it again." The crowd that was there and heard it said it had thundered; others said an angel had spoken to him. Jesus said, "This voice was for your benefit, not mine .."

In the same way, the miracle at Fatima was for the benefit of the people standing there that day, but also for the entire World. A miraculous sign was given so that we would believe the message that the children had received and then act on it.

There had been a downpour of rain just prior to the Miracle of the Sun phenomenon and so the massive crowd were soaking wet and the fields were sodden. However immediately after the inexplicable movements of the sun, observers reported that the ground and their clothing were completely dry.

De Marchi who studied the events at Fatima said: "Engineers that have studied the case reckoned that an incredible amount of energy would have been necessary to dry up those pools of water that had formed on the field in a few minutes as it was reported by witnesses."

Below is an account of the events written by Doctor Almeida Garrett, professor of the Faculty of Sciences at Coimbra university.

"It must have been 1:30 pm when there arose, at the exact spot where the children were, a column of smoke, thin, fine and bluish, which extended up to perhaps two meters above their heads, and evaporated at that height. This phenomenon, perfectly visible to the naked eye, lasted for a few seconds. Not having noted how long it had lasted, I cannot say whether it was more or less than a minute. The smoke dissipated abruptly, and after some time, it came back to occur a second time, then a third time.

"The sky, which had been overcast all day, suddenly cleared; the rain stopped and it looked as if the sun were about to fill with light the countryside that the wintery morning had made so gloomy. I was looking at the spot of the apparitions in a serene, if cold, expectation of something happening and with diminishing curiosity because a long time had passed without anything to excite my attention. The sun, a few moments before, had broken through the thick layer of clouds which hid it and now shone clearly and intensely.

"Suddenly I heard the uproar of thousands of voices, and I saw the whole multitude spread out in that vast space at my feet, turn their backs to that spot where, until then, all their expectations had been focused, and look at the sun on the other side. I turned around, too, toward the point commanding their gaze and I could see the sun, like a very clear disc, with its sharp edge, which gleamed without hurting the sight. It could not be confused with the sun seen through a fog (there was no fog at that moment), for it was neither veiled nor dim. At Fatima, it kept its light and heat, and stood out clearly in the sky, with a sharp edge, like a large gaming table. The most astonishing thing was to be able to stare at the solar disc for a long time, brilliant with light and heat, without hurting the eyes or damaging the retina. (During this time), the sun's disc did not remain immobile, it had a giddy motion, (but) not like the twinkling of a star in all its brilliance for it spun round upon itself in a mad whirl.

"During the solar phenomenon, which I have just described, there were also changes of color in the atmosphere. Looking at the sun, I noticed that everything was becoming darkened. I looked first at the nearest objects and then extended my glance further afield as far as the horizon. I saw everything had assumed an amethyst color. Objects around me, the sky and the atmosphere, were of the same color. Everything both near and far had changed, taking on the color of old yellow damask. People looked as if they were suffering from jaundice and I recall a sensation of amusement at seeing them look so ugly and unattractive. My own hand was the same color.

"Then, suddenly, one heard a clamor, a cry of anguish breaking from all the people. The sun, whirling wildly, seemed all at once to loosen itself from the firmament and, blood red, advance threateningly upon the earth as if to crush us with its huge and fiery weight. The sensation during those moments was truly terrible.

"All the phenomena which I have described were observed by me in a calm and serene state of mind without any emotional disturbance. It is for others to interpret and explain them. Finally, I must declare that never, before or after October 13 (1917), have I observed similar atmospheric or solar phenomena."

Doctor Domingos Pinto Coelho wrote an article on the event for the Ordem newspaper:

"The sun, at one moment surrounded with scarlet flame, at another aureoled in yellow and deep purple, seemed to be in an exceedingly swift and whirling movement, at times appearing to be loosened from the sky and to be approaching the earth, strongly radiating heat."

The Reverend Joaquin Laurenco also described what he saw that day, when he was a boy living in Alburitel, eighteen kilometres from Fatima:

"I feel incapable of describing what I saw. I looked fixedly at the sun, which seemed pale and did not hurt my eyes. Looking like a ball of snow, revolving on itself, it suddenly seemed to come down in a zig-zag, menacing the earth. Terrified, I ran and hid myself among the people, who were weeping and expecting the end of the world at any moment."

Alfredo de Silva Santos was also present that day and wrote:

"When Lucia called out, 'Look at the sun!' the whole multitude echoed, 'Look at the sun!' It was a day of incessant drizzle but a few moments before the miracle it left off raining. I can hardly find words to describe what followed. The sun began to move and at a certain moment appeared to be detached from the sky and about to hurtle on us like a wheel of flame. My wife – we had been married only a short time – fainted. I fell on my knees oblivious of everything and when I got up I don't know what I said. I think I began to cry out like the others."

Avelino de Almeida wrote an article about it in the Seculo newspaper:

"The sun trembled, made sudden incredible movements outside all cosmic laws – the sun 'danced' according to the typical expression of the people. They began to ask each other what they had seen. The great majority admitted to having seen the trembling and the dancing of the sun; others affirmed that they saw the face of the Blessed Virgin; others, again, saw that the sun whirled on itself like a giant catherine wheel and that it lowered itself to the earth as if to burn it in its rays. Some said they saw it change colours successively.

An article on the phenomenon was also printed in the O Dia newspaper on 17th October 1917:

At one o' clock in the afternoon, midday by the sun, the rain stopped. The sky, pearly grey in colour, illuminated the vast arid landscape with a strange light. The sun had a transparent gauzy veil so that the eyes could easily be fixed upon it. The grey mother-of-pearl tone turned into a sheet of silver which broke up as the clouds were torn apart and the silver sun, enveloped in the same gauzy grey light, was seen to whirl and turn in the circle of broken clouds. A cry went up from every mouth and people fell on their knees on the muddy ground. The light turned a beautiful blue as if it had come through the stained-glass windows of a cathedral and spread itself over the people who knelt with outstretched hands. The blue faded slowly and then the light seemed to pass through yellow glass. Yellow stains fell against white handkerchiefs, against the dark skirts of the women. They were repeated on the trees, on the stones and on the serra. People wept and prayed with uncovered heads in the presence of the miracle they had awaited. The seconds seemed like hours, so vivid were they.

Another person at the Cova da Iria that day was Dona Maria do Carmo da Cruz Menezes who said:

"Suddenly the rain stopped and the sun broke through, casting its rays on the earth. It seemed to be falling on that vast crowd of people and it spun like a fire-wheel, taking on all the colours of the rainbow. We ourselves took on those colours, with our clothes and even the earth itself. One heard cries and saw many people in tears. Deeply impressed, I said to myself: 'My God, how great is your power!'"

Bishop da Silva who was the Bishop of Leiria Fatima, wrote the following:

'The children had foretold the day and the hour at which the solar phenomenon would occur. The news spread rapidly throughout Portugal and in spite of bad weather thousands and thousands of people congregated at the spot. At the hour of the last Apparition they witnessed all the manifestations of the sun which paid homage to the Queen of Heaven and earth, more brilliant than the heavenly body itself at its zenith of light. This phenomenon, which was not registered in any astronomical observatory, and could not, therefore, have been of natural origin, was witnessed by people of every category and class, by believers as well as unbelievers, journalists of the principal daily papers and even by people kilometres away, a fact which destroys any theory of collective hallucination."

Just one month after the miracle of the sun, the Russian Civil War began and Lenin's Bolshevics or Red Army, under Trotsky, fought against their own countrymen, the White Russians, for the next three years. During this mayhem the Russian royal family were kept under house arrest at Tobolsk in Siberia, until Lenin ordered their execution on 16th July 1918.

Poland invaded the Ukraine in 1920 and fought against the Red Army until the Treaty of Riga ended the war on 18th March 1921. This brought ten million white Russians under Polish control, but the Bolshevics had won the civil war and Russia had now become a communist state.

But at this final visit to the Cova da Iria, Our Lady had said that the war would soon end and World War I did indeed end on 11th November the following year, when the armistice was signed.

(At Lourdes Our Lady also worked a miracle so that the crowds would believe, when she asked Bernadette to scratch the ground with her hands at the 9th apparition on 25th February 1858. Water miraculously emerged at this very spot and would ultimately become a spring, with an output of some 100,000 litres per day!)

News of the miracle of the sun spread like wildfire and resulted in massive numbers of people visiting the site. Some of them erected some wooden poles to form an arch and suspended lanterns from it, which they ensured were always lit. The local Government disapproved of what was happening and ordered that the arch be dismantled and that the Holm oak be removed. Whether the men carrying out these instructions did it deliberately or not, we will never know, but it was the wrong tree that was removed and Lucia was greatly relieved at this. On 6th August 1918, the feast of the Transfiguration, the locals began to build a chapel on the site of the apparitions, just as Our Lady had asked.

-Chapter 4-
Two more saints in heaven

It's incredible that Lucia's own mother still had doubts about the apparitions even after the miracle of the sun, but sometime later she became seriously ill and appeared to be close to death. Lucia and her siblings gathered around her bed and one by one they said their last goodbyes to her. As Lucia left the bedroom her two older sisters came to her saying, "Lucia! If it is true that you saw Our Lady, go right now to the Cova da Iria, and ask her to cure our mother. Promise her whatever you wish and we'll do it; and then we'll believe."

Lucia left immediately and went to the Cova, saying the Rosary as she went and at the site of the apparitions she cried and prayed that Our Lady would heal her poor mother. She said that if her mother was cured then she would visit the site every day for nine consecutive days with her sisters. They would walk on their knees from the road to the Holm oak and pray the Rosary there together. She promised that on the ninth day they would find nine poor children to take with them to the Holm oak to pray and they would give them a meal afterwards. A miracle was indeed worked and Maria came back from death's door and went on to make a full recovery.

From January 1918 until December 1920 there was an influenza pandemic which is estimated to have killed at least 50 million people worldwide, or 3% of the Earth's population. Some estimates are as high as 100 million deaths. As an example of the scale of the outbreak, 17 million people died in India, representing 5% of the entire population and on the island of Fiji 14% of the population died in just two weeks.

In 1918 the major World powers of Britain, Germany, France and the USA censored their press on what they could print on the pandemic, in order to preserve morale at home. However in Spain, which was neutral, the press reported freely and this gave the impression that the outbreak was far worse there than anywhere else and so it was referred to as 'Spanish flu.'

Research by virologists at St Bartholomew's hospital and the Royal London hospital indicated that the outbreak actually centered on the town of Etaples near Boulogne in France. It's thought that the precursor virus of this lethal strain was the H1N1 (Avian flu) virus found in birds. Etaples was a staging post for troop deployment at the end of World War I and there were very large numbers of chickens in close proximity to pigs in order to supply food for the troops.

The H1N1 virus is thought to have mutated in the pigs and was then able to cross the species barrier and pass on to man as a sub type of the Avian flu virus. It's thought that Spanish flu killed even more people than the Black Death and the majority of the deaths resulted from a secondary bacterial (not viral) pneumonia that developed under the suppressed immune system conditions. The mortality rate was at least 10%. Unfortunately at this time in history there were no immunisations to prevent the influenza infection, nor were there antibiotics to control the secondary bacterial infections, such as bacterial pneumonia.

Various researchers had noticed that Penicillium fungal moulds had an inhibitory effect on the development of bacteria, including Alexander Fleming, a Scottish biologist. In 1928 he noticed that some of his Staphylococcus culture trays had been contaminated by a blue-green mould. There was a ring around the fungal mould which was preventing the Staphylococcus bacteria from advancing beyond it. He grew a pure culture of the mould, which he identified as Penicillium notatum and over the next twelve years he grew and distributed the mould. However it was not until 1941 that large scale production of stable Penicillin was possible, in order to treat bacterial infections.

After the apparition of 13th October 1917, Francisco had said to Lucia: "I loved seeing Our Lord, but I loved still more seeing Him in that light where we were with Him as well. It's not long now, and Our Lord will take me up close to Him, and then I can look at Him forever."

He would increasingly wander off on his own to pray and to offer small sacrifices to Jesus. Lucia and Jacinta would usually find him at one of his favourite haunts, often by the side of the well. Jacinta's focus was on the conversion of sinners and trying to save people from going to Hell, but Francisco was always concerned with consoling Jesus and Our Lady through his prayers and sacrifices. Francisco was also empathetic to the sufferings of the sick people he met and often prayed for them as well.

When they were on their way to school in Fatima, Francisco sometimes urged Lucia to go on ahead, saying that he would prefer to stay with the 'hidden Jesus' in the church all day. He said there was no point in him learning how to read, as he would be going to Heaven very soon anyway. Lucia would find him still there on her way home from school several hours later.

Francisco fell ill with the Spanish flu in late October 1918 and he spent over five months suffering from its' effects. On some days when he could hardly walk he still somehow made it to the church to be with the 'hidden Jesus' and he would wait there until Lucia returned on her way back from school. When he was too ill to even get out of bed Lucia would often visit him and sometimes she would ask if he was suffering a great deal.

He would reply, "Quite a lot, but never mind! I am suffering to console Our Lord, and afterwards, within a short time, I am going to Heaven!"

While in bed he was often visited by people with petitions. One of these was from a woman from Alqueidao who asked him to pray for her friend who was gravely ill and also for the conversion of another person she knew who had fallen into sin. Although very ill himself, Francisco agreed to pray for them.

Francisco died on 4th April 1919 aged just ten and both of his parents noted that he had died with a smile on his face. Two days earlier he had made his first confession and he made his first communion the very next day, the day before he died. He was overjoyed at receiving communion and that day Jacinta and Lucia spent most of the day with him by his bedside. Lucia said her final goodbye to Francisco that night and she said to him, "Goodbye, Francisco! If you go to Heaven tonight, don't forget me when you get there, do you hear me?"

"No, I won't forget. Be sure of that," he replied. They were both crying and holding each other's hands as she said, "Goodbye then Francisco! Till we meet in Heaven, goodbye!"

Francisco died the following day and he was originally buried in the cemetery at Fatima. Shortly after his burial the lady from Alqueidao came to Lucia and Jacinta asking them to take her to his grave, to give thanks for her petitions which had both been answered!

Unfortunately Lucia's father later became ill himself and he died of double pneumonia on the 31st of July 1919. The man who had stood by Lucia and defended her, when others were verbally abusing her and the man who had bravely held Lucia's hand as they walked through a crowd of 70,000 before the miracle of the sun, was now gone.

Lucia was devastated by this loss and she said this about her father: 'He was the only one who never failed to show himself to be my friend, and the only one who defended me when disputes arose at home on account of me.'

Jacinta had also contracted the flu, about a month before Francisco and she suffered from bronchial pneumonia and abscesses on the membrane (pleura) covering the lungs. Lucia recalled in her third memoir, which was written in Tuy in 1941, the extraordinary faith that the eight year old Jacinta had.

Shortly before Jacinta was admitted to hospital she said to Lucia:

"It will not be long now before I go to Heaven. You will remain here to make known that God wishes to establish in the world devotion to the Immaculate Heart of Mary.

When you are to say this, don't go and hide. Tell everybody that God grants us graces through the Immaculate heart of Mary; that people are to ask her for them; and that the Heart of Jesus wants the Immaculate Heart of Mary to be venerated at His side. Tell them also to pray to the Immaculate Heart of Mary for peace since God has entrusted it to her.

If I could only put into the hearts of all, the fire that is burning within my own heart, and that makes me love the Hearts of Jesus and Mary so very much!"

She spent two months in St Augustine's hospital at Ourem without her family, although her mother and Lucia were sometimes able to visit her there. By the end of August 1918 her condition had deteriorated and she now had tuberculosis and pleurisy. The treatment wasn't working and the poor family could no longer afford to pay the costs and so she was taken back to Aljustrel.

By now she looked like a living skeleton as bacteria had eaten away at her body tissues but the brave eight year old said to Lucia that she was offering her sufferings for the conversion of sinners. She would also kiss the crucifix and say, "O my Jesus! I love You, and I want to suffer very much for love of You. O Jesus! Now you can convert many sinners, because this is really a big sacrifice!"

Jacinta said that Our Lady had appeared to her during her suffering to give her comfort on a number of occasions. She explained to Lucia what Our Lady had said to her on one of these visits:

"I am going to Lisbon to another hospital; I will not see you again, nor my parents either, and after suffering a great deal, I shall die alone. But she said I must not be afraid, since she herself is coming to take me to heaven."

In January 1920 Jacinta was placed in an orphanage in Lisbon appropriately named Our Lady of the Miracles and here she received Holy Communion every day, which was a great comfort to her. On the 2nd of February Jacinta was taken to the Dona Estafania hospital where she had an operation which involved making an insertion in her side to drain off the pus from two of her ribs.

She had this operation without a general anaesthetic and Doctor Leonardo who conducted the procedure was impressed with the bravery of the nine year old girl. However her condition worsened and on 20th February 1920 Jacinta made her confession in the morning and passed away later that night.

Jacinta was for a time buried in the grounds of Vila Nova de Ourem, but in 1935 her body was interred in the same mausoleum that held Francisco's remains in Fatima. When her coffin was opened in 1935 her face was found to be incorrupt and undecayed.

On the 1st of May 1951 Jacinta's remains were moved to the Basilica in Fatima and again, thirty one years after she had died, her face was found to be undecayed and incorrupt.

Francisco's small coffin was found and when it was opened he had the bone rosary beads he had been buried with still around his finger bones. His remains were then buried in the basilica on the 13th of March 1952.

-Chapter 5-

Further apparitions of Our Lady and Jesus

These were very testing times for Lucia because since the appearance of Our Lady and the miracle of the sun on 13th October 1917, she had lost the three people she cared most about. Francisco, her father and young Jacinta had all died within a period of only two years and four months of the miracle.

Lucia's mother decided to go to Lisbon for a time and here she stayed with a lady named Dona Assuncao Avelar. Dona kindly offered to pay for Lucia's education at a boarding school, but before attending this school she briefly returned to the town of Aljustrel.

On the 25th of July 1920 Bishop Jose da Silva was installed as the new Bishop of Leiria-Fatima. Jose would hold this office until 1957 and would play a very important role in ensuring that the events at Fatima were communicated effectively through to the Vatican. It was Bishop da Silva who would later declare that the visions of the children were indeed 'worthy of belief.'

On Thursday **16th June 1921** Our Lady again appeared to Lucia who was now fourteen, with a private message which has never been made public. This was just before she left for the convent school in Vilar near Porto, which was a college run by the Dorothean sisters and here she used the name Maria dos Dores, or Mary of the Sorrows. After her schooling had finished she then went to Pontevedra in Spain as a novice in the Dorothean Convent.

On the 29th of July 1921 Adolph Hitler became the leader of the National Socialist Party in Germany, the Nazi's. Back in Fatima the little chapel or Capelinha at the site of the apparitions was blown up with dynamite by enemies of the Catholic Church on 6th March 1922. However the villagers were undeterred by this and they soon rebuilt it, with the first mass being celebrated there in January 1924.

Adolph Hitler attempted to seize power in Munich in a coup on the 8th and 9th of November 1923, but his 2000 strong mob were defeated and Hitler was then arrested. He was sentenced to 5 years in prison but ultimately only served 9 months, before being released on 20th December 1924. During his imprisonment he dictated the text for his book 'Mein Kampf' to his fellow prisoner, Rudolf Hess and the book was published on the 18th of July 1925.

It was in her room at the Dorothean convent on the **10th of December 1925** that Our Lady again appeared to Lucia and in this apparition she appeared with the child Jesus by her side and Jesus was supported by a luminous cloud. Our Lady showed her a heart encircled by thorns, which she held in her hand.

The child Jesus said, "Have compassion on the Heart of your Most Holy Mother, covered with thorns, with which ungrateful men pierce it at every moment, and there is no one to make an act of reparation to remove them."

Our Lady then said:

"Look, my daughter, at my Heart, surrounded with thorns with which ungrateful men pierce me at every moment by their blasphemies and ingratitude. You can at least try to console me and say that I promise to assist at the hour of death, with the graces necessary for salvation, all those who, for five consecutive months, shall confess, receive Holy Communion, recite five decades of the Rosary, and keep me company for fifteen minutes while meditating on the fifteen mysteries of the Rosary, with the intention of making reparation to me."

Lucia wrote that Jesus again appeared to her two months later in the convent garden at Pontevedra on **15th February 1926** which she described as follows:

"On the 15th (of February 1926), I was very busy with my chores, and I scarcely thought of it (the apparition of the preceding December 10). I was about to empty the garbage can outside the garden. At the same place, several months previously, I had met a child whom I had asked if he knew the Hail Mary. He had replied yes, and I had asked him to say it for me, in order to hear him. But as he would not say it alone, I had recited it three times with him.

At the end of the three Hail Mary's, I asked him to say it alone. As he remained silent and did not appear capable of saying it alone, I asked him if he knew the church of Saint Mary. He answered yes. I then told him to go there every day and to pray thus: 'Oh my Heavenly Mother, give me Your Child Jesus!' I taught him that prayer and departed. Then on February 15, while returning as usual (to empty a garbage can outside of the garden), I found there a child who appeared to me to be the same (as previously), and I then asked him: 'Have you asked Our Heavenly Mother for the Child Jesus?'

The Child turned to me and said: 'And have you revealed to the world what the Heavenly Mother has asked you?' And saying that, He transformed Himself into a resplendent Child.

Recognising then that it was Jesus, I said to Him:

'My Jesus! You know very well what my confessor said to me in the letter I read to you. He said that this vision had to be repeated, there had to be facts permitting us to believe it, and that the Mother Superior alone could not spread this devotion.'

'It is true that the Mother Superior, alone, can do nothing, but with My grace, she can do anything. It is enough that your confessor gives you permission, and that your Superior announces this for it to be believed by the people, even if they do not know who it was revealed to.'

'But my confessor said in his letter that this devotion already exists in the world, because many souls receive Thee every first Saturday of the month, in honor of Our Lady and the fifteen mysteries of the Rosary.'

'It is true, My daughter, that many souls begin, but few persevere to the very end, and those who persevere do it to receive the graces promised. The souls who make the five first Saturdays with fervor and to make reparation to the Heart of your Heavenly Mother, please Me more than those who make fifteen, but are lukewarm and indifferent.'

'My Jesus! Many souls find it difficult to confess on Saturday. Will You allow a confession within eight days to be valid?'

'Yes. It can even be made later on, provided that the souls are in the state of grace when they receive Me on the first Saturday, and that they had the intention of making reparation to the Sacred Heart of Mary.'

'My Jesus! And those who forget to form this intention?'

'They can form it at the next confession, taking advantage of their first opportunity to go to confession.' After that the Child Jesus disappeared without saying anything more."

Lucia was soon moved to the Dorothean novitiate in Tuy which is near Pontevedra, where she finally made her vows on 3rd October 1928.

Then on **13th June 1929** she was again visited by Our Lady and this fulfilled the promise made twelve years earlier on 13th July 1917 when Our Lady had said that she would come to ask for the consecration of Russia. This is how Lucia described the encounter:

"(June 13, 1929). I had requested and obtained permission from my superiors and my confessor to make a holy hour from 11:00 p.m. to midnight, from Thursday to Friday of each week. Finding myself alone one night, I knelt down near the Communion rail, in the middle of the chapel, to recite the prayers of the Angel, lying prostrate ... Feeling tired, I got up and continued to recite them with my arms in the form of a cross. The only light was that of the (sanctuary) lamp.

Suddenly, the whole chapel lit up with a supernatural light and on the altar appeared a cross of light which reached the ceiling. In a clearer light, on the upper part of the cross, could be seen the face of a man with His body to the waist, on His chest a dove, equally luminous; and nailed to the cross, the body of another man. A little below the waist (of Christ on the cross), suspended in the air, could be seen a Chalice and a large Host, onto which some drops of Blood were falling, which flowed from the face of the Crucified One and from the wound in His breast. Running down over the Host, these drops fell into the Chalice.

Under the right arm of the cross was Our Lady with Her Immaculate Heart in Her hand ... (She appeared as Our Lady of Fatima, with Her Immaculate Heart in Her left hand, without sword or roses, but with a crown of thorns and flames) under the left arm (of the cross), in large letters, like crystalline water which flowed over the altar, forming these words: "Grace and Mercy". I understood that the mystery of the Most Holy Trinity was shown to me, and I received lights about this mystery which I am not permitted to reveal. Then Our Lady said to me:

'**The moment has come in which God asks the Holy Father to make, in union with all the bishops of the world, the consecration of Russia to My Immaculate Heart, promising to save it by this means. So numerous are the souls which the justice of God condemns for sins committed against Me, that I come to ask for reparation. Sacrifice yourself for this intention and pray.'**

I rendered an account of this to my confessor, who ordered me to write down what Our Lord willed to be done."

On the 29th of October 1929 an overheated Wall Street stock market crashed and this day came to be known as Black Tuesday and would mark the start of the great depression which lasted for ten long years.

While at Tuy, Lucia's confessor was Father Goncalves and he had given her a list of questions that he hoped she could obtain answers for, in the event of another apparition taking place. The fourth question was: "Why five Saturdays, and not nine, or seven in honour of the sorrows of Our Lady?"

On the feast of the ascension, Thursday **29th May 1930**, Lucia was given the answer to this question and she described that encounter with Our Lord Jesus and His answer as follows:

"When I was in the chapel with Our Lord part of the night of May 29-30, 1930 and I spoke to Our Lord about questions four and five, I suddenly felt myself more intimately possessed by the Divine Presence and, if I am not mistaken, this is what was revealed to me:

'My daughter, the reason is simple. There are five types of offenses and blasphemies committed against the Immaculate Heart of Mary:

Blasphemies against the Immaculate Conception.

Blasphemies against Her Perpetual Virginity.

Blasphemies against Her Divine Maternity, in refusing at the same time to recognise Her as the Mother of men.

The blasphemies of those who publicly seek to sow in the hearts of children indifference or scorn, or even hatred of this Immaculate Mother.

The offences of those who outrage Her directly in Her holy images.

Here, My daughter, is the reason why the Immaculate Heart of Mary inspired Me to ask for this little act of Reparation ...'

See, My daughter, the motive for which the Immaculate Heart of Mary inspired Me to ask for this little Reparation, and in consideration of it, to move My mercy to pardon souls who have had the misfortune of offending Her. As for you, always seek by your prayers and sacrifices to move My mercy to pity for these poor souls.'"

There was a lengthy canonical enquiry into the apparitions and the miracle of the sun at Fatima and finally on **13th October 1930** the events at Fatima were declared 'worthy of belief' by Bishop da Silva, the Bishop of Leiria-Fatima. This was seventeen years to the day, after the miracle of the sun was witnessed by tens of thousands of onlookers. Also in 1930 a papal indulgence was granted to all pilgrims visiting Fatima, but it's quite incredible that over two million people had already visited the town in the first ten years after the apparitions of 1917.

The next encounter Lucia had with Jesus was in **August 1931** at a chapel in Rianjo, near Pontevedra in Spain where Lucia had been staying with her friend as she recovered from an illness. She subsequently wrote to her Bishop describing what Jesus had said regarding the consecration of Russia. "Later, through an intimate communication, Our Lord complained to me:

'They did not wish to heed My request! ... Like the King of France they will repent of it, and they will do it, but it will be too late. Russia will have already spread its errors in the world, provoking wars and persecutions against the Church. The Holy Father will have much to suffer.'

It's thought that the reference to the King of France was referring to the revelation given to King Louis XIV by Margaret Mary Alacoque that he should publically consecrate France to the Sacred Heart of Jesus. This revelation was given to Louis XIV on the 17th of June 1689 but he failed to comply with the request.

The consecration was also not made by his son Louis XV or by his grandson Louis XVI when they came to power. One hundred years to the day after Margaret Mary Alacoque had made the request known to the King and on the Feast of the Sacred Heart, 17th June 1789, the French Revolution began. Louis XVI was stripped of his legislative power by the National Assembly and he was later guillotined on 21st January 1793. Marie Antoinette was also executed nine months later on 16th October 1793 at Place de la Concorde in Paris.

Margaret Mary was a Catholic nun and mystic who was ultimately canonized on 13th May 1920 by Pope Benedict XV. She was given several revelations over a period of 18 months from 27th December 1673 onwards and three of them were incorporated into Church practice. These are the devotion of receiving communion on the first nine Fridays, the Eucharistic adoration during a holy hour on Thursdays and the Feast of The Sacred Heart.

On the 30th of January 1933 Adolph Hitler became Chancellor of Germany and just six weeks later on the 12th of March the first concentration camp was opened at Oranienburg outside Berlin. In May of that year there was a communal burning of Jewish and 'un-German' literature outside the Berlin Opera House. President Hindenburg died on the 2nd of August 1934 and Hitler then became Fuhrer of Germany on the 19th of that month.

Lucia took her final vows as a Dorothean sister in Tuy on 3rd October 1934 and Maria Rosa was there with her on this special day. This would be the last time she would see her mother, who passed away about eight years later on 16th July 1942, which is the feast date of Our Lady of Carmel.

At the third appearance of Our Lady at the Cova da Iria on 13th July 1917, she had said that if people did not cease offending God then a worse war (than the current World War I) would break out.

She said that the sign that this was about to happen would be the phenomenon of a night being illumined by an unknown light. Amazingly Our Lady even cited the name of the Pope who would be head of the Church at that time, Pius XI. In July 1917 Ambrogio Achille Ratti, who would become Pius XI, was a lowly prefect of the library in the Vatican!

These were her specific words on that day:

'You have seen hell where the souls of poor sinners go. To save them, God wishes to establish in the world devotion to my Immaculate Heart. If what I say to you is done, many souls will be saved and there will be peace. The war is going to end; but if people do not cease offending God, a worse one will break out during the pontificate of Pius XI. When you see a night illumined by an unknown light, know that this is the great sign given you by God that He is about to punish the world for its crimes, by means of war, famine and persecutions of the Church and of the Holy Father.

To prevent this, I shall come to ask for the consecration of Russia to my Immaculate Heart, and the Communion of Reparation on the First

Saturdays. If my requests are heeded, Russia will be converted, and there will be peace; if not, she will spread her errors throughout the world, causing wars and persecutions of the Church. The good will be martyred, the Holy Father will have much to suffer, various nations will be annihilated.

In the end, my Immaculate Heart will triumph. The Holy Father will consecrate Russia to me, and she will be converted, and a period of peace will be granted to the world. In Portugal, the dogma of the faith will always be preserved ..'"

So Our Lady offered two specific remedies to prevent the outbreak of another World War from happening and to ensure peace prevailed. The first request was for the establishment of the practice of devotion to her Immaculate Heart, through the Communion of Reparation on the First Five Saturdays. The specifics of this request were given to Lucia when Our Lady appeared with the child Jesus on 10th December 1925.

Secondly, at the Cova da Iria on 13th July 1917, Our Lady had said that she would return to ask for the consecration of Russia to her Immaculate Heart and she did this on her appearance to Lucia on 13th June 1929. On this day she specifically asked that this consecration be done by the Holy Father **in union with the Bishops of the world.**

Pius XI was elected to the papacy on the 6th of February 1922 and held this office until his sudden death on the 10th of February 1939. In 1935 he canonised Thomas More, four hundred years after his death. More had opposed the protestant theology of Martin Luther as well as King Henry VIII's split from the Catholic Church and was tried for treason and beheaded.

Pius XI also canonised Don Bosco, who had started the Salesian Society for the care and education of orphans and deprived children. By the time of Don Bosco's death in 1888 there were 250 Salesian Houses catering for 130,000 children worldwide and each year about 18,000 completed their apprenticeships.

-Chapter 6-
Outbreak of World War II

In Germany on 15th September 1935 two new racial laws were passed which came to be known as the Nuremberg laws. These were the Reich Citizenship Law and the Law to Protect German Blood and Honor. They decreed that only Aryans could be full German citizens and it then became illegal for Aryans and Jews to marry.

Fascism was also on the rise in Italy and Spain and civil war broke out in Spain on the 18th of July 1936. During this rise of fascism, Pius XI was outspoken in his criticism of Nazism in general and specifically of Adolph Hitler and also of Benito Mussolini.

Then on the **25th of January 1938** the warning that Our Lady had given, of a night where the sky would be illumined by an 'unknown light' was seen throughout Europe. It was filmed, widely reported in the press and detected by astronomical observatories throughout the continent.

Scientists described the phenomenon as an unusually brilliant Aurora Borealis, the most spectacular of the 20th century, and it was also differentiated from other Aurora Borealis events by how far south it extended. It was seen clearly in Sicily, in Gibraltar and even in Madeira (32.6 degrees N).

Across the Atlantic it was visible in Bermuda (32.3 degrees N) and in the United States mainland it was observed as far south as San Diego in Southern California. The Aurora also disrupted short wave length radio signal waves from Maine to London and this is how The Times newspaper reported the event the next day:

'A remarkable and very beautiful appearance of the Aurora Borealis, or Northern Lights, was seen last night from many parts of England, including the South, where the spectacle is seldom to be seen. The display began soon after sunset, and faded and recurred for varying periods over different areas of the country till a late hour. On the Downs of the South and West, on moors and hillsides in the North, on seaside cliffs, and on the higher ground of the outskirts of London, thousands of people gathered to watch the phenomenon. A pilot of an aeroplane crossing the channel circled a number of times at several thousand feet to give his passengers an unique opportunity of seeing it...'

The article continued: 'The glow, predominantly red in the sky as seen from parts of Sussex, suggested to many people, who left their homes at first in some alarm, the reflection of a great fire. From some points the phenomenon was observed continuously for some hours.'

The report ended with: 'A Deal fisherman who returned to port last night said: "It appeared as if the whole heavens were on fire, and great beams of red light like steps stretched across the sky."

Fire brigades were called out in Austria and Switzerland to attend to suspected fires, because the sky appeared as a flaming red curtain. In Budapest in Hungary the phenomenon lasted intermittently for about six hours and news reporters recorded the event in Munich and as far south as Gibraltar. Fishermen in Ostend were so concerned about the significance of the phenomenon that they remained in port that night. Along the Pyrenees in villages near the frontier, the Aurora caused panic as the villagers thought it was the result of aerial bombardment in Spain.

Another newspaper reported: 'The Aurora, which has not been seen in Portugal for 50 years, was observed throughout the country for more than two and a half hours. It went on: 'Our Gibraltar correspondent states that the Aurora there took the form of streamers, arches, and patches of varying colour and shade, and offered a magnificent sight. It has not been seen at Gibraltar within living memory. The phenomenon was also visible in many districts of Italy, particularly Piedmont and Venetia. At Rome it appeared twice, and at Catania, in Sicily, three times.'

A correspondent in Vienna wrote: 'Yesterday's Aurora brought almost the whole population of Vienna into the streets, the cafés being emptier while it lasted longer than at any time in living history.'

Just six weeks after this spectacular event, Hitler annexed Austria on 12th March 1938 and later that year he annexed the Sudetenland border regions of Czechoslovakia. The land grab by Germany and a new era of war with the most terrible consequences, had effectively begun.

50

On the 9th and 10th of November 1938, thousands of Nazis attacked and burned hundreds of synagogues. Thousands of Jewish homes, schools and businesses were also attacked and about one hundred Jews were killed in the night known as Kristallnacht, the night of broken glass. Shortly after this about 30,000 Jewish men were arrested and taken to one of three Nazi concentration camps.

By 1939 Jews were not permitted to attend school or to hold public positions in either Germany or Italy and they were also barred from working as lawyers or doctors. Pope Pius XI had been vociferous in his criticism of fascism and the appalling treatment of the Jews in Germany and Italy. He intended to make a stinging rebuke of Nazism and fascism with his Bishops in an encyclical he would pronounce on the 11th of February 1939, three months after Kristallnacht.

By this time reports had reached Mussolini that the pope may be about to excommunicate him, a move which would have severely damaged his (and Hitler's) support base in the general population. The Pope mysteriously died on 10th February 1939 the day before he was to release the encyclical, apparently due to a heart attack.

He was buried in the grotto of Saint Peter's Basilica in the Apostolic Palace. The Pope had bravely stood up against Nazism and had defended the rights of the Jews right up until the day he died. He had indeed suffered much!

Eugenio Pacelli who was consecrated as a Bishop on 13th May 1917, the very day of the first apparition, was elected to the papacy as Pius XII on the 2nd of March 1939.

On the **19th of March 1939**, Lucia wrote:

"Whether the world has war or peace depends on the practice of this devotion, along with the consecration to the Immaculate Heart of Mary. This is why I desire its propagation so ardently, especially because this is also the will of our dear Mother in Heaven."

Lucia was clearly concerned that Our Lady's requests were still not being heeded and on **20th June 1939** she wrote again:

"Our Lady promised to put off the scourge of war, if this devotion was propagated and practiced. We see that She will obtain remission of this chastisement to the extent that efforts are made to propagate this devotion; but I fear that we can do more than we are doing and that

51

God, being displeased, will pull back the arm of His mercy and let the world be ravaged by this chastisement which will be unlike any other in the past, horrible, horrible."

Ten weeks later on **1st September 1939** Germany invaded Poland and Britain's Prime Minister Neville Chamberlain declared war on Germany two days later.

Our Lady had asked for the Holy Father, in union with the bishops of the World, to consecrate Russia to her Immaculate Heart at Tuy on 13th June 1929. On that visitation she asked again for reparation to be made for the sins committed against her Immaculate Heart i.e. the communion of reparation on the first five Saturdays. This was ten full years before the outbreak of World War II.

Lucia said that when Our Lord appeared to her at the chapel in Rianjo in August 1931, He had complained that they had still not acted on Our Lady's requests and had warned of the consequences of this. This was eight years before the outbreak of war! Lucia played her part and immediately wrote to her bishop advising him of the revelation she had received. Unfortunately Our Lady's requests were consistently ignored and the Second World War had now begun.

On the 2nd of December 1940 Lucia wrote to the new pope, Pius XII regarding Our Lady's request for the pope, in union with the Bishops of the World, to consecrate Russia to her Immaculate Heart. She was clearly concerned that all her requests for the consecration of Russia and the First Five Saturdays devotion to Our Lady, were not being acted upon.

By now Germany had occupied Poland; France; Denmark; Finland; Norway; Belgium; Luxembourg; Holland, Czechoslovakia and Romania. Germany had also signed a non aggression pact with Russia on the 23rd of August 1939. On the 10th of May 1940 Winston Churchill had become Prime Minister and one month later, on the 10th of June, Italy also declared war on Britain.

On the 10th of July of that year the Battle of Britain would begin. This would be the largest aerial battle in history and resulted in the loss of about 1023 British fighter planes and 1887 German bombers and fighters. Some 544 British pilots and 2500 German aircrew were killed in the battle, which raged until the end of October 1940 and the Blitz of London would kill about 40,000 civilians.

The war in North Africa was also underway as well as the Battle for the Atlantic, with massive numbers of U-Boats attacking naval vessels and supply ships. These were dark days indeed for the World and it's no wonder that Lucia felt it necessary to appeal yet again to the pope, to action Our Lady's requests. She wrote:

Most Holy Father,

Humbly prostrated at your feet, I come as the last sheep of the fold entrusted to you to open my heart, by order of my spiritual director.

I am the only survivor of the children to whom our Lady appeared in Fátima (Portugal) from the 13th of May to the 13th of October 1917. The Blessed Virgin has granted me many graces, the greatest of all being my admission to the Institute of Saint Dorothy.

I come, Most Holy Father, to renew a request that has already been brought to you several times. The request, Most Holy Father, is from our Lord and our good Mother in Heaven.

In 1917, in the portion of the apparitions that we have designated 'the secret,' the Blessed Virgin revealed the end of the war that was then afflicting Europe, and predicted another forthcoming, saying that to prevent it She would come and ask the consecration of Russia to Her Immaculate Heart as well as the Communion of reparation on the first Saturday. She promised peace and the conversion of that nation if Her request was attended to.

She announced that otherwise this nation would spread her errors throughout the world, and there would be wars, persecutions of the Holy Church, martyrdom of many Christians, several persecutions and sufferings reserved for Your Holiness, and the annihilation of several nations.

Most Holy Father, this remained a secret until 1926 according to the express will of our Lady. Then, in a revelation She asked that the Communion of reparation on the first Saturdays of five consecutive months be propagated throughout the world, with its conditions of doing the following with the same purpose; going to confession, meditating for a quarter of an hour on the mysteries of the Rosary and saying the Rosary with the aim of making reparation for the insults, sacrileges and indifferences committed against Her Immaculate Heart.

Our good Heavenly Mother promises to assist the persons who practise this devotion, in the hour of their death, with all the necessary graces for their salvation. I exposed the request of our Lady to my confessor, who tried to have it fulfilled, but only on the 13th of September 1939 did His Excellency the Bishop of Leiria make public in Fatima this request of our Lady.

I take this opportunity, Most Holy Father, to ask you to bless and extend this devotion to the whole world. In 1929, through another apparition, our Lady asked for the consecration of Russia to Her Immaculate Heart, promising its conversion through this means and the hindering of the propagation of its errors.

Sometime afterwards I told my confessor of the request of our Lady. He tried to fulfill it by making it known to Pius XI.

In several intimate communications our Lord has not stopped insisting on this request, promising lately, to shorten the days of tribulation which He has determined to punish the nations for their crimes, through war, famine and several persecutions of the Holy Church and Your Holiness, if you will consecrate the world to the Immaculate Heart of Mary, with a special mention for Russia, and order that all the Bishops of the world do the same in union with Your Holiness.

I truly feel your sufferings, Most Holy Father! And, as much as I can through my humble prayers and sacrifices, I try to lessen them, close to our Lord and the Immaculate Heart of Mary.

Most Holy Father, if in the union of my soul with God I have not been deceived, our Lord promises a special protection to our country in this war, due to the consecration of the nation by the Portuguese Prelates, to the Immaculate Heart of Mary; as proof of the graces that would have been granted to other nations, had they also consecrated themselves to Her.

Now, Most Holy Father, allow me to make one more request, which is but an ardent wish of my humble heart; that the feast in honour of the Immaculate Heart of Mary be extended throughout the whole world as one of the main feasts of the Holy Church.

With the deepest respect and reverence I ask for the Apostolic Blessing. May God protect Your Holiness.

Tuy, Spain, **2ⁿᵈ of December of 1940**. Maria Lucia de Jesus.

In June 1938, while Pius XI was still in office, there had been a written request for him to consecrate the World to the Immaculate Heart of Mary. This time the request for consecration didn't come from Lucia but from a Jesuit priest, Father Mariano Pinho and several Portuguese Bishops. The request was as a result of messages that a lady named Alexandrina Maria da Costa from Balazar in Portugal, said she had received from Jesus and the Virgin Mary.

When Alexandrina was fourteen years of age four men had attempted to break into her room to attack her and to escape she had jumped out of a window, falling thirteen feet to the ground. Her spine was broken and she suffered from a deteriorating paralysis that later confined her to bed for thirty years from 1925 until her death on the 13th of October 1955.

According to her Vatican biography, Alexandrina received no food except the Holy Eucharist each day from March 1942 onwards. Miraculously she survived without food for thirteen years!

The request by Father Pinho and the Bishops was made several times through to 1941 when Pius XII was in office and the Vatican on three occasions requested additional information about Alexandrina. Pope John Paul II would later declare Alexandrina of Balazar 'blessed' on the 25th of April 2004.

On the **13th of May 1942**, the 25th anniversary of the first apparition at Fatima, the Vatican finally published the Message and Secret of Fatima, but this did not include details of the 'third secret,' which Lucia had kept to herself.

Finally, thirteen years and four months after Our Lady's request at Tuy and three whole years into the war, Pope Pius XII did make a consecration to the Immaculate Heart of Mary.

In his radio address in Portuguese of **31st October 1942** the Pope consecrated the Church and all humanity to the Immaculate Heart of Mary, with specific mention of Russia. This is a small part of his address:

"To you, to your Immaculate Heart, we as common Father of the great Christian family, as Vicar of the One who was given all power in Heaven and on Earth, received the request of many souls redeemed with His Blood who populate the world, - to You, to Your Immaculate Heart, at this tragic time of human history we trust, we deliver, consecrate not only the Holy Church, the mystical body of Jesus, that pities and bleeds into so many pieces and by so many ways troubled, but also the entire world, torn by discord, scorched in fires of hatred, a victim of its own iniquities."

Lucia was later to comment that the consecration by Pius XII was not in accord with what Our Lady had requested, as it lacked the participation of the Bishops representing the entire body of the Faithful.

In June 1943 Lucia fell seriously ill, which greatly concened Bishop da Silva, the Bishop of Leiria-Fatima. So in October 1943 after Lucia had recovered, Canon Galamba, an advisor of Bishop da Silva suggested that the Bishop ask Lucia to commit her vision of 13th July 1917 (the third secret) to writing. Canon Galamba suggested that she could place it in an envelope sealed with wax, but only to be opened at a later date.

The Bishop clearly had concerns that should she die then the secret would die with her and he personally went to Tuy on 15th September 1943 with his request. Lucia was unhappy with this verbal request and asked that it be put in writing, which the Bishop did in mid October.

Lucia was agonising over what to do for several weeks but had another visitation by Our Lady on **2nd January 1944** to reassure her that this was indeed the will of God. Lucia subsequently wrote to Bishop da Silva on the 9th of January 1944 to advise him that she had complied with his request.

She wrote, "I have written what you asked me; God willed to try me a little, but finally, this was indeed His will: it (the third part of the Secret) is sealed in an envelope and it is in the notebooks…"

This clearly implies that the account of the vision was written down twice i.e. in the letter in the sealed envelope and also in her notebooks. Lucia had kept the vision she was given on 13th July 1917 a secret for 26 years, but it was still to remain a secret for a very long time to come!

Lucia hand delivered the envelope to Bishop Ferreira, Archbishop of Gurza, who delivered it that evening to Bishop da Silva. However the letter remained unopened at this time and it was agreed that if Bishop da Silva were to die, that the envelope would be given to Cardinal Cerejeira, the Patriarch of Lisbon.

Lucia had written on the envelope that it could only be opened **after 1960** either by the Patriarch of Lisbon or by the Bishop of Leiria.

The war in Europe ended with the surrender of Germany on the 7th of May 1945 and hostilities ended in the east with the surrender of Japan on the 2nd of September of that year. The war had directly killed about 60 million people or 2.5% of the world population. In addition to this another 19 to 25 million had died from war related famine and disease so the overall figure was between 79 and 85 million.

This war was unique in that there were massive civilian casualties estimated to have been at least 38 million people killed directly. In addition to this about 19 to 25 million civilians died of famine and disease. The war had also seen the use of nuclear weapons for the first time, with combined deaths at Hiroshima and Nagasaki estimated at a minimum of 150,000 with higher estimates being around 244,000.

Our Lady had warned us of the horror of this war and given mankind a remedy to prevent it, but the World had simply not responded.

-Chapter 7-
The third secret remains a secret

On the 25th of March 1948 Lucia entered the Carmelite Convent in Coimbra and she assumed the name Sister Maria Lucia of the Immaculate Heart.

Three years later, on the 13th of October 1951 Cardinal Tedeschini who was the Papal Legate, made the most incredible announcement. He said in his address to a crowd of one million people who were gathered at Fatima, that Pius XII had personally witnessed a repetition of the 1917 miracle of the sun while he was in the Vatican gardens.

The Pope had witnessed this event four times, on 30th October; 31st October, 1st November and 8th November 1950. The Pope promulgated the dogma of the Corporal Assumption of the Blessed Virgin Mary on the 1st of November 1950 and he took this miracle as confirmation that his plan to do so was correct.

The Pope was clearly affected by what he'd seen and spoke about the solar phenomena with some of his cardinals and close colleagues. Sister Lehnert who was in charge of the papal apartments at the time, said:

"Pius XII was very convinced of the reality of the extraordinary phenomenon, which he had seen on four occasions."

About one year and eight months after witnessing this phenomenon, Pope Pius XII consecrated Russia to the Blessed Virgin Mary. This was in his Apostolic letter 'Sacro Vergente Anno' of **7th July 1952**. The relevant text is:

"And therefore we, in order that Our and your prayers may be more easily answered, and in order to give you a special attestation of our benevolence, in the same way as a few years ago We consecrated the entire world to the immaculate Heart of the virgin Mother of God, so now, in a very special way, consecrate all peoples of Russia to the very same immaculate Heart, in the safe confidence that with the extremely powerful protection of the virgin Mary the wishes expressed by Us, by you and by every good person for a true peace for fraternal concord and due freedom for everyone and for the Church in the first place, may be answered as soon as possible; in such a manner that, through the prayer that We send up to Heaven together with you and all Christians, the reign of Christ, harbinger of salvation, which is 'kingdom of truth and life, kingdom of sainthood and grace, kingdom of justice, of love and of peace', may triumph and steadily consolidate itself everywhere on earth"

However this consecration also didn't satisfy the condition that it be made 'in union with the Bishops of the world.' Our Lady clearly wanted this consecration of Russia to be made by the entire Church on Earth and not just by the Pope himself.

In early 1957 while Pius XII was still in office, the Vatican requested that the envelope Lucia had given to Bishop da Silva on the 17th of June 1944, her notebooks and copies of all her writings at the chancery of Leiria, be sent to the Papal nuncio. So Bishop da Silva gave these documents to his auxiliary Bishop Venancio in the middle of March 1957. Venancio then took them to Bishop Cento, who was the Apostolic Nuncio to Lisbon. Lucia's letter and the other documents finally arrived at the Vatican on the **16th of April 1957** and were placed in a little chest in the office of Pius XII. Eight months later, on the **26th of December 1957** Lucia addressed Father Fuentes with these words:

'The Blessed Virgin is very sad, for no one attaches any importance to Her Message ... Neither the good nor the bad ...' 'The good continue on their way but without paying attention to the Message ... I cannot give any other details, since it is still a secret ... Only the Holy Father and His Excellency the Bishop of Fatima would be able to know it in accordance to the Will of the Blessed Virgin ... But they haven't willed to know it as they did not want to be influenced.' (Father Fuentes was Postulator of the beatification causes of Jacinta and Francisco.)

It's impossible to say whether or not Pope Pius XII ultimately intended to make the contents of the letter known to the World. After all he did have them in his possession at the Vatican for 18 months without releasing them by the time of his death on the 9th of October 1958. Apparently the envelope was never even opened by the pope. Pius XII, who had a special relationship with Our Lady, was laid to rest in the crypt of Saint Peter's Basilica on the 13th of October, which fittingly is the feast date of Our Lady of Fatima!

John XXIII took the papacy on the 28th of October 1958 and on the **17th of August 1959** the pope requested the envelope containing the third secret and this was taken to him at Castel Gandolfo by Monsignor Philippe, a Vatican official. Castel Gandolfo is a 17th century papal palace in the town of the same name and is situated about 24 kilometres southeast of Rome. It has an interesting history with popes using it as a retreat, but during World War II it gave protection to a very large number of Jewish refugees who were escaping the Nazis. Under the Lateran Treaty of 1929 it was protected as an extraterritorial property of the Holy See. Both Pius XII and Paul VI died at Castel Gandolfo. For some reason the pope didn't read the letter that same day but opened it a few days later. The Portuguese writing was translated for the pope by Monsignor Paulo Jose Tavarez and the pope also asked that it be read to Cardinal Ottaviani, who was the Prefect of the Holy Office.

By 1960 there was a great expectation that the third secret would finally be made public. Close to six months after the secret had been read by Pope John XXIII and his two associates, a press statement by the Vatican was released on the **8th of February 1960**:

"Faced with the pressure that has been placed on the Vatican, some wanting the letter to be opened and made known to the world, others, on the supposition that it may contain alarming prophecies, desiring that its publication be withheld, the same Vatican circles declare that the Vatican has decided not to make public Sister Lucia's letter, and to continue keeping it rigorously sealed. The decision of the Vatican authorities is based on various reasons: 1. Sister Lucia is still living. 2. The Vatican already knows the contents of the letter. 3. Although the Church recognises the Fatima apparitions, she does not pledge herself to guarantee the veracity of the words which the three little shepherds claim to have heard from Our Lady. In these circumstances, it is most probable that the Secret of Fatima will remain, forever, under absolute seal.'

It was John XXIII who convened the Second Vatican Council which opened on the 11th of October 1962. It was actually the 21st ecumenical council but only the second council to be held at St Peter's Basilica and this council essentially addressed the relations between the Roman Catholic Church and the modern World. One of the most profound changes introduced was permission to say the mass in the vernacular instead of Latin. John XXIII died on the 3rd of June 1963 in the Apostolic Palace of the Vatican City.

Pope Paul VI took office on the 21st of June 1963 and on the **21st of November 1964** he renewed the consecration of the World to the Immaculate Heart of Mary. This was done with the Bishops present at the close of the third session of the Second Vatican Council, but it was not done with their participation and again Russia was not specifically named in the consecration. In his address the Pope proclaimed The Most Blessed Mary as Mother of the Church and he also placed the whole Church under the protection of Our Lady of Fatima. The part of his address containing the words of consecration are given below:

"While We turn in ardent prayer to the Virgin, that she may bless the Ecumenical Council and the entire Church, hastening the hour of union of all Christians, Our glance opens on the endless horizons of the whole world, the object of the most lively care of the Ecumenical Council, and which Our venerated predecessor, Pius XII of venerated memory, not without inspiration from on high, solemnly Consecrated to the Immaculate Heart of Mary. Today, We consider it particularly opportune to recall this act of Consecration. Bearing this in mind, We have decided to send a special mission to Fatima in the near future in order to carry the Golden Rose to the sanctuary of Fatima, more dear than ever not only to the people of the noble Portuguese nation - always, but particularly today, dear to Us - but also known and venerated by the faithful throughout the entire Catholic world. In this manner We intend to entrust to the care of this heavenly Mother the entire human family, with its problems and anxieties, with its legitimate aspirations and ardent hopes."

The Pope finally read Lucia's letter on the **27th of March 1965** with Archbishop Angelo Dell'Acqua but decided not to publish the third secret and the letter was returned to the Vatican archives. However he did endorse official Church support for Fatima by making his own pilgrimage there on the 13th of May 1967. This was the 50th anniversary of the first apparition and he prayed together with Lucia at the shrine. Pope Paul VI died on the 6th of August 1978 and was succeeded by John Paul I (born Albino Luciani) who only held the papacy for 33 days until his death at the age of sixty five on the 28th of September 1978. John Paul I was the first Pope to take a double name and the first to do away with the coronation ceremony for a new Pope.

-Chapter 8-
The consecration of Russia and the World

On Wednesday **13th of May 1981**, the anniversary of the first apparition at Fatima, there was an assassination attempt on Pope John Paul II. The pope was being driven very slowly through a crowd of 20,000 people, standing in an open car in St Peter's Square at about 5:15 in the afternoon. Four shots were fired from very close range, about 15 feet, and the Pope was hit in his lower intestine, right arm and left index finger. The 9mm bullets from the Browning Hi-power pistol caused severe blood loss, necessitating a transfusion of 6 pints of blood and parts of the pope's intestine had to be removed in three places. Doctor Rodolfo Proietti the chief physician who operated on the pope for five hours and twenty five minutes said, "I don't know how he survived the shooting."

The shooter, Mehmet Ali Agca was sentenced to life but was later forgiven by the pope, who famously went to visit him in prison in 1983. He was pardoned by the Italian President Carlo Ciampi at the pope's request and then deported to Turkey in June 2000. The pope would later give one of the bullets which so nearly claimed his life, to the Bishop of Leiria-Fatima on his visit to Rome. The Bishop then had the bullet set in the crown of the statue of Our Lady in the shrine at Fatima.

The pope wrote a prayer which he called 'An Act of Entrustment' to be celebrated in the Basilica of Saint Mary Major on the 7th of June 1981. As he was unable to be physically present his recorded address was broadcast instead. The part of the Act of Entrustment that clearly related to Russia, although not specifically mentioned, is given below:

"Mother of all individuals and peoples, you know all their sufferings and hopes. In your motherly heart you feel all the struggles between good and evil, between light and darkness, that convulse the world: accept the plea which we make in the Holy Spirit directly to your heart, and embrace with the love of the Mother and Handmaid of the Lord those who most await this embrace, and also those whose act of entrustment you too await in a particular way. Take under your motherly protection the whole human family, which with affectionate love we entrust to you, O Mother. May there dawn for everyone the time of peace and freedom, the time of truth, of justice and of hope."

John Paul II was absolutely convinced that Our Lady had saved his life and he asked that Lucia's letter be brought to him and this was done on the **18th of July 1981**. He was given two envelopes, a white one containing the original Portuguese text and an orange envelope containing an Italian translation. Archbishop Martinez Somalo, Substitute of the Secretariat of State handed him the envelopes. However on the 11th of August Archbishop Somalo returned the envelopes to the Vatican Archives.

Lucia wrote to the pope on the **12th of May 1982** and in the letter she explained that the fulfillment of some of the warnings in the prophecies given on the 13th of July 1917 had already come about. **This had happened because mankind had not responded to Our Lady's requests.** Furthermore Lucia warned that we may well be moving towards the fulfillment of the final part of the prophecy due to the prevalence of so much sin in the world.

We must bear in mind that Lucia's letter was written after the assassination attempt on John Paul II. In other words, that event was not the end point of the prophecy in the third secret otherwise she would not have written:

'And if we have not yet seen the complete fulfillment of the final part of this prophecy, we are going towards it little by little with great strides.'

At the third apparition the children were given a vision of Hell and Our Lady called for devotion to Her Immaculate Heart to save souls and to ensure peace. She also told the children that the current war would soon end but that if mankind did not stop offending God then a worse war would break out. She prophesied a night illumined by an unknown light would be the sign that this was about to happen. Man would be punished by war, famine, persecutions of the Church and the Holy Father.

Our Lady said that she would return to ask for two things - the consecration of Russia to Her Immaculate Heart and the Communion of reparation on the first five Saturdays. She said that if these two requests were met then there would be peace and Russia would be converted. If not, Russia would spread her errors throughout the World causing wars and persecutions of the Church. She said that the good would be martyred, the Holy Father would have much to suffer and that various nations would be annihilated. However she said that in the end her Immaculate Heart would triumph and that the Holy Father would consecrate Russia to her, and that Russia would be converted and a period of peace granted to the world.

Our Lady with the child Jesus appeared to Lucia on the 10th of December 1925 in her room at the Dorothean convent in Pontevedra. Here she asked for the Communion of Reparation on the First Five Saturdays. The child Jesus appeared to Lucia two months later in the convent garden on the 15th of February 1926, again asking for the devotion of the Communion of Reparation.

Our Lady appeared to Lucia on the 13th of June 1929 at the Dorothean Novitiate in Tuy while she was kneeling at the communion rail in the chapel. Here she called for the consecration of Russia to her Immaculate Heart to be made. However she again made a plea for the Communion of Reparation on the first five Saturdays to be observed.

These are Lucia's words in her letter of 12th May 1982 to John Paul II:

"The third part of the secret refers to Our Lady's words: 'If not (Russia) will spread her errors throughout the world, causing wars and persecutions of the Church. The good will be martyred; the Holy Father will have much to suffer; various nations will be annihilated' (13-VII-1917).

The third part of the secret is a symbolic revelation, referring to this part of the Message, conditioned by whether we accept or not what the Message itself asks of us: 'If my requests are heeded, Russia will be converted, and there will be peace; if not, she will spread her errors throughout the world, etc.'

Since we did not heed this appeal of the Message, we see that it has been fulfilled, Russia has invaded the world with her errors. And if we have not yet seen the complete fulfillment of the final part of this prophecy, we are going towards it little by little with great strides. If we do not reject the path of sin, hatred, revenge, injustice, violations of the rights of the human person, immorality and violence, etc.

And let us not say that it is God who is punishing us in this way; on the contrary it is people themselves who are preparing their own punishment. In his kindness God warns us and calls us to the right path, while respecting the freedom he has given us; hence people are responsible".

Exactly one year after the assassination attempt, the pope visited Fatima on the 13th of May 1982 and after a concelebrated mass he consecrated the whole world to the Immaculate Heart of Mary. This is part of his address:

'We have recourse to your protection, holy Mother of God.' As I utter the words of this antiphon with which the Church of Christ has prayed for centuries, I find myself today in this place chosen by you, O Mother, and by you particularly loved. I am here, united with all the Pastors of the Church in that particular bond whereby we constitute a body and a college, just as Christ desired the Apostles to be in union with Peter. In the bond of this union, I utter the words of the present Act, in which I wish to include, once more, the hopes and anxieties of the Church in the modern world.

Forty years ago and again ten years later, your servant Pope Pius XII, having before his eyes the painful experience of the human family, entrusted and consecrated to your Immaculate Heart the whole world, especially the peoples for which you had particular love and solicitude. This world of individuals and nations I too have before my eyes today, as I renew the entrusting and consecration carried out by my Predecessor in the See of Peter: the world of the second millennium that is drawing to a close, the modern world, our world today!

The Church, mindful of the Lord's words: 'Go... and make disciples of all nations... and lo, I am with you always, to the close of the age' (Mt 28:19-20), renewed, at the Second Vatican Council, her awareness of her mission in this world.

And therefore, O Mother of individuals and peoples, you who 'know all their sufferings - and their hopes', you who have a mother's awareness of all the struggles between good and evil, between light and darkness, which afflict the modern world, accept the cry which we, as though moved by the Holy Spirit, address directly to your Heart. Embrace, with the love of the Mother and Handmaid, this human world of ours, which we entrust and consecrate to you, for we are full of disquiet for the earthly and eternal destiny of individuals and peoples. In a special way we entrust and consecrate to you those individuals and nations which particularly need to be entrusted and consecrated. We have recourse to your protection, holy Mother of God: reject not the prayers we send up to you in our necessities."

The Pope ended his address with these words which specifically covered the areas of war (including nuclear war); abortion, injustice in society and atheism.

"In entrusting to you, O Mother, the world, all individuals and peoples, we also entrust to you the consecration itself, for the world's sake, placing it in your motherly Heart.

Oh, Immaculate Heart! Help us to conquer the menace of evil, which so easily takes root in the hearts of the people of today, and whose immeasurable effects already weigh down upon our modern world and seem to block the paths towards the future!

From famine and war, deliver us.

From nuclear war, from incalculable self-destruction, from every kind of war, deliver us.

From sins against the life of man from its very beginning, deliver us.

From hatred and from the demeaning of the dignity of the children of God, deliver us.

From every kind of injustice in the life of society, both national and international, deliver us.

From readiness to trample on the commandments of God, deliver us.

From attempts to stifle in human hearts the very truth of God, deliver us.

From sins against the Holy Spirit, deliver us, deliver us.

Accept, O Mother of Christ, this cry laden with the sufferings of all individual human beings, laden with the sufferings of whole societies.

Let there be revealed, once more in the history of the world your infinite power of merciful Love. May it put a stop to evil. May it transform consciences. May your Immaculate Heart reveal for all the light of Hope."

Although Russia was again not mentioned specifically, the words 'In a special way we entrust and consecrate to you those individuals and nations which particularly need to be entrusted and consecrated' were clearly referring to Russia.

The Pope had invited all the Bishops to join him in the consecration but many had not received the invitation by the 13th of May 1982. So the consecration did not involve all the world's bishops and again Sister Lucia said that it did not fulfill the request of Our Lady.

During his homily at the mass he celebrated on that day the pope said:

"The Message is addressed to every human being. ... Because of the continuing increase of sin and the dangers, such as nuclear war, now threatening humanity, the Message of Fatima is more urgent and relevant in our time than it was when Our Lady appeared 65 years ago."

He also said: "Today John Paul II, successor of St. Peter, presents himself before the Mother of the Son of God in Her shrine at Fatima. In what way does he come? He presents himself reading again with trepidation the motherly call to penance, to conversion, the ardent appeal of the Heart of Mary that resounded at Fatima 65 years ago. Yes he reads it again with trepidation in his heart because he sees how many people and societies - how many Christians - have gone in the opposite direction to the one indicated in the Message of Fatima. Sin has thus made itself firmly at home in the world, and denial of God has become widespread in the ideologies, ideas and plans of human beings."

In October 1983 at the synod of Bishops, John Paul II renewed the consecration that he had made the previous year. The subject of this synod was 'Penance and Reconciliation in the Mission of the Church' and the commentary of this synod is well worth reading. The synod ran from 29th September until 29th October 1983.

Finally on the **25th of March 1984** John Paul II renewed the 1982 consecration that he had made at Fatima and this time the Bishops had been notified that their participation was required, well in advance. The pope had requested that the statue of Our Lady of Fatima be brought to Rome for the occasion. This was the feast of the Annunciation and the Pope made the consecration on his knees before the statue of Our

Lady of Fatima, which is the same statue venerated in the Chapel of the Apparitions.

Again the text didn't mention Russia specifically, but the Pope did reference the acts of consecration made by Pope Pius XII in 1942 and 1952. The 1952 consecration was essentially concerned with Russia. It also appears that John Paul II paused at times during the ceremony and according to the Bishop of Leiria-Fatima, Alberto Cosme do Amaral, he quietly included Russia in the consecration wording.

So finally Russia was consecrated to the Immaculate Heart of Mary, but what of Our Lady's other request – the establishment of devotion to Her Immaculate Heart through the Communion of Reparation on the first five Saturdays? It's unfortunately clear that the World has simply ignored this request of Our Lady.

Debate continues in some quarters to this day as to whether or not even the 25th of March 1984 consecration satisfied the conditions set out by Our Lady. However the Apostolic Nuncio visited Sister Lucia after this consecration and she is reported to have confirmed that the 1984 consecration did indeed satisfy the request of Our Lady.

In October 1989 an interview with Sister Lucia was published in the Fatima Family Messenger and in it she said that the Apostolic Nuncio had asked her, "Is Russia now consecrated?"

She said that she had replied, "Yes, now it is."

Then the interviewer asked, "Now we wait for the miracle?" to which she replied, "God will keep His word."

Lucia also wrote another letter on the 8th of November 1989 which was subsequently published in the March 1990 edition of the Catholic publication '30 days.' Regarding the consecration of Russia she wrote:

"It was later made by the present Pontiff, John Paul II, on 25th March 1984, after he wrote to all the Bishops of the World, asking that each of them make the consecration in his own diocese with the people of God who had been entrusted to him. The Pope asked that the statue of Our Lady of Fatima be brought to Rome and he did it publicly in union with all the bishops who, with His Holiness, were uniting themselves with the people of God, the Mystical Body of Christ; and it was made to the Immaculate Heart of Mary, Mother of Christ and of His mystical body, so that, with her and through her with Christ, the consecration could be carried and offered to the Father for the salvation of humanity. Thus the consecration was made by His Holiness Pope John Paul II on 25th March 1984."

The next year, on the 3rd of July 1990 Lucia wrote a letter to Rev. Father Robert J. Fox and in it she again confirmed that Our Lady's request regarding the consecration of Russia had been achieved.

She wrote: "I come to answer your question, 'If the consecration made by Pope John Paul II on March 25, 1984 in union with all the bishops of the world, accomplished the conditions for the consecration of Russia according to the request of Our Lady in Tuy on June 13 of 1929?' Yes, it was accomplished, and since then I have said that it was made. And I say that no other person responds for me, it is I who receive and open all letters and respond to them."

Archbishop Tarcisio Bertone also issued a statement in 2001 claiming that during a meeting with Sister Lucia on the 17th of November of that year she had told him, "I have already said that the consecration desired by Our Lady was made in 1984, and has been accepted in Heaven."

Tarcisio Bertone was at that time the Secretary of the Congregation for the Doctrine of the Faith. Sister Lucia was 94 at the time and the meeting was conducted in the presence of the prioress of St Teresa's Carmelite Convent. Also present at the meeting that afternoon was Father Luis Kondor who was vice postulator of the cause of Blessed Francisco and Jacinta.

Lucia was also asked whether it was true that the concerns she had were robbing her of her sleep and that she was praying night and day. She apparently responded, "It's not true. How would I be able to pray during the day if I did not sleep at night? How many things they attribute to me! How many things they make me do! They should read my book; the advice and appeals that correspond to Our Lady's wishes are there. "Prayer and penance, with great faith in God's power, will save the world."

Surely the message of Fatima is encapsulated by these two words - **Prayer and Penance**.

-Chapter 9-
Third secret made public

Pope John Paul II made his second pilgrimage to Fatima from 10th to 13th May 1991 and again made an act of entrustment of the World to the mother of God. Then on the 13th of May 2000, Lucia at the age of ninety-three was at Fatima to witness Pope John Paul II beatify Jacinta and Francisco. Jacinta is the youngest non-martyred child to have been beatified in the Church.

It's incredible that even by this time the third secret of Fatima had still not been released to the World. However John Paul II had now decided that the time was right for the revelations to be made public. Prior to the release of the third secret the pope wrote to Sister Lucia on the 19th of April 2000 to say that he was sending Archbishop Tarcisio Bertone, the Secretary for the Doctrine of the Faith, as well as the Bishop of Leiria-Fatima to meet with her and to ask certain questions about the interpretation of the secret.

The meeting took place eight days later on the **27th of April 2000** in the Carmel of Saint Teresa in Coimbra. Lucia was handed the two envelopes and she opened the white one and read the letter and then confirmed that it was her handwriting. The letter in Portuguese was read and translated by the Bishop of Leiria-Fatima and Lucia said that she agreed with the translation.

She said that the vision of Fatima was above all concerned with the struggle of atheistic Communism against the Church and against Christians, and described the terrible sufferings of the victims of faith in the twentieth century.

She was asked, "Is the principal figure in the vision the Pope?" and she replied that it was. Lucia also confirmed that the children at Fatima had believed that the 'Bishop dressed in white' in the vision was indeed the Holy Father.

Lucia also said that she fully agreed with what John Paul II had said, that 'it was a mother's hand that guided the bullet's path enabling the Pope in his throes to halt at the threshold of death.' The Pope had written this in his Meditation from the Policlinico Gemelli to the Italian Bishops on the 13th of May 1994.

Archbishop Bertone asked Lucia why she had said that the letter could only be opened after 1960 and if it was Our Lady who had fixed that date. Lucia replied: "It was not Our Lady. I fixed the date because I had the intuition that before 1960 it would not be understood, but that only later would it be understood. Now it can be better understood. I wrote down what I saw; however it was not for me to interpret it, but for the Pope."

At the end of the meeting Lucia was presented with a rosary from the Holy Father and she in turn gave some of her hand made rosaries to the ambassadors, to give to Pope John Paul II. A few weeks later on the 13th of May 2000 the pope was in Fatima for the beatification of Jacinta and Francisco. This was his third visit to Fatima and at the end of the mass he took the opportunity to ask Cardinal Sodano to make a statement about the third secret without revealing much detail:

"Brothers and Sisters in the Lord! At the conclusion of this solemn celebration, I feel bound to offer our beloved Holy Father Pope John Paul II, on behalf of all present, heartfelt good wishes for his approaching 80th Birthday and to thank him for his vital pastoral ministry for the good of all God's Holy Church; we present the heartfelt wishes of the whole Church.

On this solemn occasion of his visit to Fatima, His Holiness has directed me to make an announcement to you. As you know, the purpose of his visit to Fatima has been to beatify the two 'little shepherds.' Nevertheless he also wishes his pilgrimage to be a renewed gesture of gratitude to Our Lady for her protection during these years of his papacy. This protection seems also to be linked to the so-called third part of the 'secret' of Fatima.

That text contains a prophetic vision similar to those found in Sacred Scripture, which do not describe photographically the details of future events, but synthesise and compress against a single background facts which extend through time in an unspecified succession and duration. As a result, the text must be interpreted in a symbolic key.

The vision of Fatima concerns above all the war waged by atheistic systems against the Church and Christians, and it describes the immense suffering endured by the witnesses of the faith in the last century of the second millennium. It is an interminable Way of the Cross led by the Popes of the twentieth century.

According to the interpretation of the 'little shepherds', which was also confirmed recently by Sister Lucia, 'the Bishop clothed in white' who prays for all the faithful is the Pope. As he makes his way with great difficulty towards the Cross amid the corpses of those who were martyred (Bishops, priests, men and women Religious and many lay people), he too falls to the ground, apparently dead, under a hail of gunfire.

After the assassination attempt of 13 May 1981, it appeared evident that it was 'a mother's hand that guided the bullet's path, enabling the Pope in his throes to halt at the threshold of death.' On the occasion of a visit to Rome by the then Bishop of Leiria-Fatima, the Pope decided to give him the bullet which had remained in the jeep after the assassination attempt, so that it might be kept in the shrine. By the Bishop's decision, the bullet was later set in the crown of the statue of Our Lady of Fatima.

The successive events of 1989 led, both in the Soviet Union and in a number of countries of Eastern Europe, to the fall of the Communist regimes which promoted atheism. For this too His Holiness offers heartfelt thanks to the Most Holy Virgin. In other parts of the world, however, attacks against the Church and against Christians, with the burden of suffering they bring, tragically continue.

Even if the events to which the third part of the 'secret' of Fatima refers now seem part of the past, Our Lady's call to conversion and penance, issued at the start of the twentieth century, remains timely and urgent today.

'The Lady of the message seems to read the signs of the times - the signs of our time - with special insight. The insistent invitation of Mary Most Holy to penance is nothing but the manifestation of her maternal concern for the fate of the human family, in need of conversion and forgiveness.'

In order that the faithful may better receive the message of Our Lady of Fatima, the Pope has charged the Congregation for the Doctrine of the Faith with making public the third part of the 'secret', after the preparation of an appropriate commentary.

Brothers and Sisters, let us thank Our Lady of Fatima for her protection. To her maternal intercession let us entrust the Church of the Third Millennium."

On the **26th of June 2000**, about eighty three years after Lucia had been given the vision, the Vatican finally released the text of the third secret as contained in Lucia's letter, which is given below:

'I write in obedience to you, my God, who command me to do so through his Excellency the Bishop of Leiria and through your Most Holy Mother and mine.

After the two parts which I have already explained, at the left of Our Lady and a little above, we saw an Angel with a flaming sword in his left hand; flashing, it gave out flames that looked as though they would set the world on fire; but they died out in contact with the splendour that Our Lady radiated towards him from her right hand: pointing to the earth with his right hand, the Angel cried out in a loud voice: 'Penance, Penance, Penance!'

And we saw in an immense light that is God: 'something similar to how people appear in a mirror when they pass in front of it' a Bishop dressed in White 'we had the impression that it was the Holy Father'. Other Bishops, Priests, men and women Religious going up a steep mountain, at the top of which there was a big Cross of rough-hewn trunks as of a cork-tree with the bark; before reaching there the Holy Father passed through a big city half in ruins and half trembling with halting step, afflicted with pain and sorrow, he prayed for the souls of the corpses he met on his way; having reached the top of the mountain, on his knees at the foot of the big Cross he was killed by a group of soldiers who fired bullets and arrows at him, and in the same way there died one after another the other Bishops, Priests, men and women Religious, and various lay people of different ranks and positions. Beneath the two arms of the Cross there were two Angels each with a crystal aspersorium in his hand, in which they gathered up the blood of the Martyrs and with it sprinkled the souls that were making their way to God.'

Along with the text of the letter, a theological commentary on this vision was released by Cardinal Ratzinger, the Prefect of the Congregation for the Doctrine of the Faith. Cardinal Ratzinger would become Pope Benedict XVI on the 19th of April 2005. His commentary read:

"A careful reading of the text of the so-called third "secret" of Fatima, published here in its entirety long after the fact and by decision of the Holy Father, will probably prove disappointing or surprising after all the speculation it has stirred. No great mystery is revealed; nor is the future unveiled.

We see the Church of the martyrs of the century which has just passed represented in a scene described in a language which is symbolic and not easy to decipher. Is this what the Mother of the Lord wished to communicate to Christianity and to humanity at a time of great difficulty and distress? Is it of any help to us at the beginning of the new millennium? Or are these only projections of the inner world of children, brought up in a climate of profound piety but shaken at the same time by the tempests which threatened their own time? How should we understand the vision? What are we to make of it?

The first and second parts of the "secret" of Fatima have already been so amply discussed in the relative literature that there is no need to deal with them again here. I would just like to recall briefly the most significant point. For one terrible moment, the children were given a vision of hell. They saw the fall of "the souls of poor sinners". And now they are told why they have been exposed to this moment: "in order to save souls"- to show the way to salvation.

The words of the First Letter of Peter come to mind: "As the outcome of your faith you obtain the salvation of your souls" (1:9).

To reach this goal, the way indicated - surprisingly for people from the Anglo-Saxon and German cultural world - is devotion to the Immaculate Heart of Mary. A brief comment may suffice to explain this. In biblical language, the "heart" indicates the centre of human life, the point where reason, will, temperament and sensitivity converge, where the person finds his unity and his interior orientation. According to Matthew 5:8, the 'immaculate heart' is a heart which, with God's grace, has come to perfect interior unity and therefore 'sees God'.

To be 'devoted' to the Immaculate Heart of Mary means therefore to embrace this attitude of heart, which makes the fiat – 'your will be done' - the defining centre of one's whole life. It might be objected that we should not place a human being between ourselves and Christ. But then we remember that Paul did not hesitate to say to his communities: 'imitate me' (1 Cor 4:16; Phil 3:17; 1 Th 1:6; 2 Th 3:7, 9). In the Apostle they could see concretely what it meant to follow Christ. But from whom might we better learn in every age than from the 'Mother of the Lord.'

Thus we come finally to the third part of the "secret" of Fatima which for the first time is being published in its entirety. As is clear from the documentation presented here, the interpretation offered by Cardinal Sodano in his statement of 13 May was first put personally to Sister Lucia. Sister Lucia responded by pointing out that she had received the vision but not its interpretation.

The interpretation, she said, belonged not to the visionary but to the Church. After reading the text, however, she said that this interpretation corresponded to what she had experienced and that on her part she thought the interpretation correct. In what follows, therefore, we can only attempt to provide a deeper foundation for this interpretation, on the basis of the criteria already considered.

'To save souls' has emerged as the key word of the first and second parts of the 'secret', and the key word of this third part is the threefold cry: 'Penance, Penance, Penance!' The beginning of the Gospel comes to mind: "Repent and believe the Good News" (Mk 1:15).

To understand the signs of the times means to accept the urgency of penance - of conversion - of faith. This is the correct response to this moment of history, characterised by the grave perils outlined in the images that follow. Allow me to add here a personal recollection: in a conversation with me Sister Lucia said that it appeared ever more clearly to her that the purpose of all the apparitions was to help people to grow more and more in faith, hope and love - everything else was intended to lead to this.

Let us now examine more closely the single images. The angel with the flaming sword on the left of the Mother of God recalls similar images in the Book of Revelation. This represents the threat of judgement which looms over the world. Today the prospect that the world might be reduced to ashes by a sea of fire no longer seems pure fantasy: man himself, with his inventions, has forged the flaming sword.

The vision then shows the power which stands opposed to the force of destruction - the splendour of the Mother of God and, stemming from this in a certain way, the summons to penance.

In this way, the importance of human freedom is underlined: the future is not in fact unchangeably set, and the image which the children saw is in no way a film preview of a future in which nothing can be changed. Indeed, the whole point of the vision is to bring freedom onto the scene and to steer freedom in a positive direction.

The purpose of the vision is not to show a film of an irrevocably fixed future. Its meaning is exactly the opposite: it is meant to mobilise the forces of change in the right direction. Therefore we must totally discount fatalistic explanations of the 'secret', such as, for example, the claim that the would-be assassin of 13 May 1981 was merely an instrument of the divine plan guided by Providence and could not therefore have acted freely, or other similar ideas in circulation. Rather, the vision speaks of dangers and how we might be saved from them.

The next phrases of the text show very clearly once again the symbolic character of the vision: God remains immeasurable, and is the light which surpasses every vision of ours. Human persons appear as in a mirror. We must always keep in mind the limits in the vision itself, which here are indicated visually. The future appears only 'in a mirror dimly' (1 Cor 13:12).

Let us now consider the individual images which follow in the text of the 'secret'. The place of the action is described in three symbols: a steep mountain, a great city reduced to ruins and finally a large rough-hewn cross. The mountain and city symbolise the arena of human history: history as an arduous ascent to the summit, history as the arena of human creativity and social harmony, but at the same time a place of destruction, where man actually destroys the fruits of his own work.

The city can be the place of communion and progress, but also of danger and the most extreme menace. On the mountain stands the cross - the goal and guide of history. The cross transforms destruction into salvation; it stands as a sign of history's misery but also as a promise for history.

At this point human persons appear: the Bishop dressed in white ('we had the impression that it was the Holy Father'), other Bishops, priests, men and women Religious, and men and women of different ranks and social positions. The Pope seems to precede the others, trembling and suffering because of all the horrors around him. Not only do the houses of the city lie half in ruins, but he makes his way among the corpses of the dead.

The Church's path is thus described as a Via Crucis, as a journey through a time of violence, destruction and persecution. The history of an entire century can be seen represented in this image. Just as the places of the earth are synthetically described in the two images of the mountain and the city, and are directed towards the cross, so too time is presented in a compressed way. In the vision we can recognise the last century as a century of martyrs, a century of suffering and persecution for the Church, a century of World Wars and the many local wars which filled the last fifty years and have inflicted unprecedented forms of cruelty.

In the 'mirror' of this vision we see passing before us the witnesses of the faith decade by decade. Here it would be appropriate to mention a phrase from the letter which Sister Lucia wrote to the Holy Father on 12 May 1982: 'The third part of the 'secret' refers to Our Lady's words: 'If not, (Russia) will spread her errors throughout the world, causing wars and persecutions of the Church. The good will be martyred; the Holy Father will have much to suffer; various nations will be annihilated'".

In the Via Crucis of an entire century, the figure of the Pope has a special role. In his arduous ascent of the mountain we can undoubtedly see a convergence of different Popes. Beginning from Pius X up to the present Pope, they all shared the sufferings of the century and strove to go forward through all the anguish along the path which leads to the Cross.

In the vision, the Pope too is killed along with the martyrs. When, after the attempted assassination on 13 May 1981, the Holy Father had the text of the third part of the 'secret' brought to him, was it not inevitable that he should see in it his own fate? He had been very close to death, and he himself explained his survival in the following words: '... it was a mother's hand that guided the bullet's path and in his throes the Pope halted at the threshold of death" (13 May 1994).

That here 'a mother's hand' had deflected the fateful bullet only shows once more that there is no immutable destiny, that faith and prayer are forces which can influence history and that in the end prayer is more powerful than bullets and faith more powerful than armies.

The concluding part of the 'secret' uses images which Lucia may have seen in devotional books and which draw their inspiration from long-standing intuitions of faith. It is a consoling vision, which seeks to open a history of blood and tears to the healing power of God. Beneath the arms of the cross angels gather up the blood of the martyrs, and with it they give life to the souls making their way to God.

Here, the blood of Christ and the blood of the martyrs are considered as one: the blood of the martyrs runs down from the arms of the cross. The martyrs die in communion with the Passion of Christ, and their death becomes one with his. For the sake of the body of Christ, they complete what is still lacking in his afflictions (Col 1:24). Their life has itself become a Eucharist, part of the mystery of the grain of wheat which in dying yields abundant fruit. The blood of the martyrs is the seed of Christians, said Tertullian. As from Christ's death, from his wounded side, the Church was born, so the death of the witnesses is fruitful for the future life of the Church.

Therefore, the vision of the third part of the 'secret', so distressing at first, concludes with an image of hope: no suffering is in vain, and it is a suffering Church, a Church of martyrs, which becomes a sign-post for man in his search for God.

The loving arms of God welcome not only those who suffer like Lazarus, who found great solace there and mysteriously represents Christ, who wished to become for us the poor Lazarus. There is something more: from the suffering of the witnesses there comes a purifying and renewing power, because their suffering is the actualisation of the suffering of Christ himself and a communication in the here and now of its saving effect.

And so we come to the final question: What is the meaning of the 'secret' of Fatima as a whole (in its three parts)? What does it say to us? First of all we must affirm with Cardinal Sodano: '... the events to which the third part of the 'secret' of Fatima refers now seem part of the past'.

Insofar as individual events are described, they belong to the past. Those who expected exciting apocalyptic revelations about the end of the world or the future course of history are bound to be disappointed. Fatima does not satisfy our curiosity in this way, just as Christian faith in general cannot be reduced to an object of mere curiosity. What remains was already evident when we began our reflections on the text of the 'secret': the exhortation to prayer as the path of 'salvation for souls' and, likewise the summons to penance and conversion.

I would like finally to mention another key expression of the 'secret' which has become justly famous: 'my Immaculate Heart will triumph'. What does this mean? The Heart open to God, purified by contemplation of God, is stronger than guns and weapons of every kind. The fiat of Mary, the word of her heart, has changed the history of the world, because it brought the Saviour into the world - because, thanks to her Yes, God could become man in our world and remains so for all time.

The Evil One has power in this world, as we see and experience continually; he has power because our freedom continually lets itself be led away from God. But since God himself took a human heart and has thus steered human freedom towards what is good, the freedom to choose evil no longer has the last word. From that time forth, the word that prevails is this: 'In the world you will have tribulation, but take heart; I have overcome the world' (Jn 16:33). The message of Fatima invites us to trust in this promise."

John Paul II had the original statue of Our Lady of Fatima brought to the Vatican on the 8th of October 2000 and he entrusted the new millennium to Mary in front of 1500 bishops from around the World.

Lucia passed away at the age of ninety-seven on Sunday the 13th of February 2005 in the company of the Carmelite sisters of her convent where she had lived for about 57 years. The Bishop of Coimbra was also present with her when she died.

Pope Benedict XVI visited Fatima on the 12th and 13th of May 2010 and he said that 'he was bringing the problems and sufferings of the world to Fatima.' Benedict was there to celebrate the 10th anniversary of the beatification of Jacinta and Francisco and at the mass he celebrated, he also marked the anniversary of the apparitions, as well as the 1981 assassination attempt on John Paul II.

While he was at the shrine he again affirmed that John Paul firmly believed that the Virgin's unseen hand had rescued him from death in the assassination attempt. Benedict also said to Our Lady: "It is a profound consolation to know that you are crowned not only with the silver and gold of our joys and hopes but also with the 'bullet' of our anxieties and sufferings."

It's interesting that while he was on his way to Portugal, Pope Benedict was asked if the suffering of John Paul II contained in Fatima's third secret could be extended to encompass the suffering of the church today concerning the clerical abuse scandal. Benedict affirmed that it could, arguing that the Fatima message doesn't respond to a particular situation or time but offers a 'fundamental response' to the constant need for penance and prayer.

Pope Francis mentioned the statue of Our Lady of Fatima in his very first Angelus prayer on Sunday the 17th of March 2013 and he also asked Cardinal Policarpo to consecrate his pontificate to Our Lady of Fatima. This was carried out on the 13th of May 2013 which was the 96th anniversary of the first apparition of Our Lady at Fatima.

The Pope had the statue of Our Lady of Fatima brought to the Vatican on Saturday 12th October and he led a vigil that night in St Peter's square. Many in the crowd held their own replica statues as the statue from Fatima was carried through the square.

The next day, Sunday the 13th of October, Pope Francis entrusted the world to Our Lady in front of a crowd of 100,000 people who had gathered in the square. This was the date of the anniversary of the last apparition at Fatima.

-Chapter 10-
Our Lady's role as intercessor

God found it necessary to make a direct intervention in the pathway of development of mankind some two thousand years ago. He had sent many prophets over a period of one and a half millennia, from the time of Moses through to the latter day prophets such as Zechariah, in an attempt to draw man from sin and to His love and to true spirituality. We are after all spiritual beings living in a material world and unfortunately the response to the message of these prophets was at best short lived.

Moses had been given two stone tablets inscribed with the Ten Commandments on Mount Sinai. However the practical interpretation of these had evolved by the time of Jesus into a staggering code of 613 mitzvot or observances, of which 365 were negative rules and 248 were positive instructions. So Jewish Law or Halakha had largely replaced spirituality and although a highly devout Jew could meet most of the conditions of the mitvot, he could still fail to honour God by not showing true love for his fellow man. There was no remedy to atone for the sins of mankind and the sacrificial sin offerings offered by the High Priest in the temple would not guarantee the salvation of souls.

Left unchecked, mankind would veer ever further off the pathway to salvation and to eternal life. Sending more prophets would not present an ongoing solution and so God sent His only son into the World. It's important to remember that Jesus and the Holy Spirit existed with God the Father at the beginning of time and were involved in the creation. This is clear in the beginning of John's gospel where Jesus is called 'The Word' and also in Genesis where the words 'we' and 'us' are used and where the 'Spirit of God' is mentioned.

Genesis 1:1: In the beginning God created the heavens and the earth. Now the earth was formless and empty, darkness was over the surface of the deep, and the Spirit of God was hovering over the waters.

Genesis 1:26: Then God said, "Let us make man in our image, in our likeness ...."

John 1:1: In the beginning was the Word, and the Word was with God, and the Word was God. He was with God in the beginning. Through him all things were made; without him nothing was made that has been made.

The timing of this intervention, i.e. the Son of God coming to Earth, was critically important. Had this been done too early in man's history then the message might not have spread worldwide, as the World population would have been too low and there would have been insufficient trade links established. Had the intervention been made too late then very many more souls would not have inherited eternal life. So it made sense for Jesus to become incarnate at the time he did, because by then there were established languages, towns and international trade routes, but the world population was still low.

The history of the Israelites wandering in the desert shows us that nothing imperfect could exist with God, as is clear from Exodus.

Exodus 19:12: Put limits for the people around the mountain and tell them, 'Be careful that you do not go up the mountain or touch the foot of it. Whoever touches the mountain shall surely be put to death.'

Exodus 33:19: And the Lord said, "I will cause all my goodness to pass in front of you, and I will proclaim my name, the Lord, in your presence. I will have mercy on whom I will have mercy, and I will have compassion on whom I will have compassion. But," he said, "You cannot see my face, for no one may see me and live."

Now the Son of God could have just materialised on Earth and begun His teaching ministry and He would then have been fully and solely God. However a radical way of bringing Jesus into the World was for Him to be carried in the womb and physically born of a woman. This shows the unfathomable depths of love that God has for His creation that He was prepared to allow His Son to become totally vulnerable on Earth, to experience the full range of emotions and dangers that prevail for all of us. Despite this Jesus would remain fully God.

So how could the mutually exclusive entities of a perfect God and inherently sinful mankind be brought together to allow the Christ to exist in the womb of a woman? Quite simply this would be impossible if it were not for the unique qualities of Mary. The Church teaching of the Immaculate Conception refers to the fact that from the very moment of Mary's conception she was without sin. She had no stain of original sin and was therefore uniquely positioned to bear the Christ in her womb. Matthew's gospel mentions an angel appearing to Joseph in a dream after he had discovered that Mary, who he was engaged to, was pregnant.

Matthew 1:20: But after he had considered this, an angel of the Lord appeared to him in a dream and said, "Joseph, son of David, do not be afraid to take Mary home as your wife, because what is conceived in her is from the Holy Spirit. She will give birth to a son, and you are to give him the name Jesus, because he will save his people from their sins."

In Luke's gospel we read of the encounter Mary herself had with the angel Gabriel.

Luke 1:26: In the sixth month, God sent the angel Gabriel to Nazareth, a town in Galilee, to a virgin pledged to be married to a man named Joseph, a descendent of David. The virgin's name was Mary. The angel went to her and said, "Greetings, you who are highly favoured! The Lord is with you." Mary was greatly troubled at his words and wondered what kind of greeting this might be. But the angel said to her, "Do not be afraid, Mary, you have found favour with God. You will be with child and give birth to a son, and you are to give him the name Jesus. He will be great and will be called the Son of the Most High. The Lord God will give him the throne of his father David, and he will reign over the house of Jacob for ever; his kingdom will never end."

"How will this be," Mary asked the angel, "since I am a virgin?"

The angel answered, "The Holy Spirit will come upon you and the power of the Most High will over-shadow you. So the holy one to be born will be called the Son of God. Even Elizabeth your relative is going to have a child in her old age, and she who was said to be barren is in her sixth month. For nothing is impossible with God."

"I am the Lord's servant," Mary answered. "May it be to me as you have said." Then the angel left her.

At that time Mary got ready and hurried to a town in the hill country of Judea, where she entered Zechariah's home and greeted Elizabeth. When Elizabeth heard Mary's greeting, the baby leaped in her womb, and Elizabeth was filled with the Holy Spirit. In a loud voice she exclaimed, "Blessed are you among women, and blessed is the child you will bear!"

So between the greeting of Gabriel and the exclamation of Elizabeth we have the first part of our prayer we call the 'Hail Mary.'

The fact that the Son of God would be born to a virgin was prophesied seven hundred years earlier by Isaiah.

Isaiah 7:13: Then Isaiah said, "Hear now, you house of David! Is it not enough to try the patience of men? Will you try the patience of my God also? Therefore the Lord himself will give you a sign: The virgin will be with child and will give birth to a son, and will call him Immanuel." (meaning God with us)

As Isaiah said, this sign for mankind would not be given by a prophet but by Almighty God Himself. And so we can see the unique position that Mary occupies of all the women who have ever lived - she was completely without sin and therefore able to carry the Christ in her womb.

Mary had a difficult life starting from before she even gave birth to Jesus, having to travel from Nazareth to Bethlehem to comply with the decree issued by Caesar Augustus that a census be taken of the Roman Empire. When Jesus was eight days old Mary and Joseph took him to the temple of Jerusalem to be circumcised and they were met in the temple courts by a devout Jew named Simeon. He had been assured that he would not die until he had seen the Christ of God. Simeon took Jesus in his arms and then he blessed Mary and Joseph, saying: "This child is destined to cause the falling and rising of many in Israel, and to be a sign that will be spoken against, so that the thoughts of many hearts will be revealed. And a sword will pierce your own soul too." (Luke 2:34)

The words of Simeon about a sword piercing her soul was one of the seven dolours or sorrows that she would face and Mary would have to worry about the meaning of these words all her life. Another sorrow was when the Holy family had to flee Herod and live in Egypt for a few years, far away from their families and loved ones. The third sorrow was when Jesus went missing for four days until his distraught parents found him sitting in the temple with the teachers of the Law. The fourth sorrow was when Mary met her beloved son on his way to

Calvary, lacerated from the scourging and struggling to stay on His feet and the fifth was when Our Lady stood near the foot of the cross and watched her son Jesus die. Her sixth sorrow was to see the centurion Longinus pierce the side of Jesus with a lance and shortly after this, receiving His body into her arms. The last sorrow was to see the body of Jesus being placed in the tomb by Nicodemus and Joseph of Arimathea.

At the sixth apparition at Fatima, Our Lady appeared as Our Lady of Dolours (Sorrows) and then as Our Lady of Carmel. The Carmelite order traces its origins back to a group of Christian hermits who lived in Palestine in the early 13th century and the movement was established in Europe later that century. In England it was headed by a man named Simon Stock who Our Lady is said to have appeared to and given a brown scapular to wear. She apparently gave an assurance that those who died wearing the scapular would be saved. Simon is thought to have lived in Aylesford in Kent which is where the first general chapter of the Carmelite Order was held outside the Holy Land, in 1247. He died in the Carmelite monastery in Bordeaux in 1265 and although miracles have been attributed to him, he has yet to be canonized.

John, the disciple whom Jesus loved, was the only apostle actually present at the crucifixion and Jesus gave this disciple into the care of His mother Mary.

John 19:25: Near the cross of Jesus stood his mother, his mother's sister, Mary the wife of Clopas, and Mary Magdalene. When Jesus saw his mother there, and the disciple whom he loved standing near by, he said to his mother, "Dear woman, here is your son." And to the disciple, "Here is your mother." From that time on, this disciple took her into his home.

The depth of feeling between mother and son was plain to see at Calvary and the fact that Jesus entrusted Mary to John shows his great concern for her wellbeing. However it also shows that he fully intended Mary to be involved in the growth of the fledgling Church going forward and we can see her involvement in Acts1:14:

'They all joined together constantly in prayer, along with the women and Mary the mother of Jesus, and with his brothers.'

Jesus knew the vital role that John would play as an evangelist and as the author of his gospel and the book of Revelation. There was mutual benefit to be derived from Mary helping John and vice versa and they would both need each other's support over the rest of their lives.

No-one knew Jesus like Mary and we can only speculate about how often John must have consulted Mary before putting quill to parchment. We will also never know the wealth of knowledge that Jesus shared with his mother as he lived at home over a period of thirty years. Reading the account of the wedding at Cana it's clear that Mary already knew that Jesus could work miracles and it makes one wonder if he had performed some miracles before his public ministry began!

There are two traditions in the Church regarding where Mary died and was assumed into Heaven. One tradition holds that she died in Jerusalem, but the other places her death at Ephesus and it's generally accepted that John himself died there and was buried at nearby Selcuk, about 3 kilometres from the city. The site of where Mary may well have lived is on the slopes of the Bulbul mountain in Ephesus and is called Meryemana (The Virgin Mary's house). The original building is gone but another was rebuilt on the site and has been preserved to this day. There's a spring in the garden which many believe has been a source of healing and mass is held outdoors in the evenings.

The Emperor Domitian attempted to kill John by having him poisoned and then thrown into a cauldron of boiling oil, in front of a packed Colosseum. The execution attempt failed and he miraculously emerged unhurt from the boiling oil, which apparently resulted in a very large number of conversions to Christianity. This event was described by the ancient historian Tertullian in chapter 36 of his work, 'The prescription against heretics.' The enraged Domitian then exiled John to the penal island of Patmos, which is where he is believed to have written Revelation. However after his exile John returned to Ephesus.

So Our Lady played a unique and essential role in the Son of God becoming incarnate in our world. Mary is also our spiritual mother and is surely a perfect model of motherhood for our World. After her assumption into Heaven she has performed an ongoing role as an intercessor for us to her Son Jesus. Mary has been entrusted with this role by her son as a means of helping countless souls towards a deeper devotion of him and to eternal life.

-Chapter 11-
What is the message of Fatima?

If we examine the words of the Virgin Mary at her six appearances, we can summarise the themes as follows:

Our Lady on all six visits asked that the Rosary be prayed every day and on three of them she went further and linked this to peace in the World and the end of World War I.

On three of the visits she spoke of how offended God is by the sins of mankind and on another, that her Immaculate Heart was outraged by the sins of humanity.

On three occasions Our Lady spoke of the need for reparation for the sins that had been committed by mankind and on the second visit she held a heart which was encircled by thorns.

Our Lady spoke on three of the visits about the need for prayer and sacrifices to be made for the conversion of sinners.

She spoke of Hell and/or Purgatory on three visits and gave a terrifying vision of Hell at her third appearance. At the fourth apparition Our Lady said that, 'many souls go to Hell.'

She said on the second visit that Jesus wished to establish a devotion to her Immaculate Heart and on the third visit that God Himself wished to establish this devotion i.e. the communion of reparation on the first five Saturdays. On the second visit Our Lady gave the promise of salvation to all who embraced the First Five Saturdays devotion. She also linked this devotion and the consecration of Russia to her Immaculate Heart to peace in the World and to the salvation of souls.

At the third and fifth apparitions Our Lady promised a miracle, which was the Miracle of the Sun on the 13th of October 1917.

On the third visit Our Lady called for the consecration of Russia.

She also gave the warning that if people did not stop offending God, then a worse war would break out and she gave the sign of a night illumined by an unknown light as the sign that the World was about to be punished for its crimes.

There are clearly two central themes here – the first is the **need for repentance** and the second is the **need for prayer**. What's implicit in the words of Our Lady is that there are consequences for sin, both at the level of the individual and at the societal level. So although Jesus has given himself up as a sacrifice for our sins, this clearly does not take away the necessity for us to repent!

There are also parallels here with the message Our Lady gave to the 14 year old Bernadette Soubirous at Lourdes. On the 6th apparition on the 21st of February 1858, Bernadette asked Our Lady:

"What saddens you?"

Our Lady replied, "Pray for sinners."

On the 8th visit on the 24th of February Our Lady said:

"Penance! Penance! Penance! Pray to God for sinners."

She repeated these same words at two subsequent visits on the 27th and 28th of February 1858.

It's clear from what Our Lady said at Fatima that Jesus, God the Father, the Holy Spirit and she herself are offended and hurt, even outraged by the sins that are being committed. However God's love for His creation is so great that He desires every soul to be saved and to enjoy eternal life with Him and so He withholds the retribution that is warranted with immense patience, but ultimately there is a tipping point.

Mary linked our sins to wars, famine, disease and persecutions of the Church and showed us a remedy for this through our turning from sin, repentance and prayers. Our Lady showed that our future is not set in stone, but can be radically altered through our prayers and devotion. She herself is a remedy, if we would only embrace the devotion to Her Immaculate Heart that she asked for. Whatever prayers we make to her will be leveraged greatly to produce positive effects for us as individuals and for the entire World.

Europe and other parts of the World witnessed a night illumined by an unknown light on the 25th of January 1938 and World War II followed, so it's obvious that mankind simply failed to stop offending God through sin.

We ignored the call to repentance; to stop sinning, to establish the First Five Saturdays devotion and we were very slow to heed the call to consecrate Russia to her Immaculate Heart. Our history books show us the terrible consequences of this inaction!

So is there a message from Fatima that is relevant today and if so what can we learn from it? Firstly we need to examine what motivated Our Lady to make the appearances that she did in the first place. It was clearly out of concern for the large number of people that were in danger of going to Hell and also to warn mankind that the offences caused by sin would have terrible consequences in this earthly life too.

She gave the horrifying vision of Hell to show that this is a reality and not a myth, to shake people from their complacency and to urge them to repent. Our Lady was therefore concerned with both our earthly life and with the eternal welfare of our souls. She came to offer an effective remedy which would ensure ongoing peace in our World and the salvation of our souls.

As Pope Benedict said, the message offers a fundamental response to the **constant need for penance and prayer.** The incredible promise she gave to those who make the devotion of the first five Saturdays cannot be taken lightly – Our Lady said that she would assist at death with the graces necessary for their salvation. What more could we possibly ask for?

Unfortunately man's spiritual journey has seen two phenomena come together in our modern world. We live in a time of very great sinfulness and yet this has coincided with an unprecedented decline in repentance, at least as measured by the number of Catholics going to confession. The Centre for applied research on the Apostolate published a report in 2005 which showed that only 2% of Catholics attended confession on a regular basis and three quarters never went at all or went less than once a year.

It was in 1215 AD at the 4th Lateran Council that all Christians in the Latin Church were bound to go at least once a year for a confession and the confession had to be in private.

The concept of there being a debt for past sins is not an easy one to comprehend but it's surely in line with the laws of natural justice. In

Genesis we have the account of the Great Flood where the flood waters decimated mankind over a period of 150 days.

Genesis 6:5: The Lord saw how great man's wickedness on the earth had become, and that every inclination of the thoughts of his heart was only evil all the time. The Lord was grieved that he had made man on the earth, and his heart was filled with pain. So the Lord said, 'I will wipe mankind, whom I have created, off from the face of the earth - men and animals, and creatures that move along the ground, and the birds of the air - for I am grieved that I have made them.'

The plains cities of Sodom and Gomorrah were later destroyed as a direct consequence of the sinfulness of their inhabitants and the biblical history of the Israelites is surely an example to us of how God showed man that there were consequences for his sin.

When Moses was on Mount Sinai receiving the Decalogue from God, the Israelites rebelled and Aaron made a golden calf out of the earrings they had taken from the Egyptians. The punishment for this idolatry was that 3000 were put to death by the Levites and God also punished the people with a plague.

Later Moses returned to the mountain where he spent forty days in the presence of God, fasting all the time, and he was again given the Ten Commandments. God made a covenant with man on this basis, as is clear from Exodus 34:27:

Then the Lord said to Moses, 'Write down these words, for in accordance with these words I have made a covenant with you and with Israel.' Moses was there with the Lord forty days and forty nights without eating bread or drinking water. And he wrote on the tablets the words of the covenant - the Ten Commandments.

Jesus himself warned us of the consequences of sin and that there was a debt that had to be accounted for.

Matthew 12:34: 'For out of the overflow of the heart the mouth speaks. The good man brings good things out of the good stored up in him, and the evil man brings evil things out of the evil stored up in him. But I tell you that men will have to give account on the Day of Judgment for every careless word they have spoken. For by your words you will be acquitted, and by your words you will be condemned.'

Matthew 5:25: 'Settle matters quickly with your adversary who is taking you to court. Do it while you are still with him on the way, or he may hand you over to the judge, and the judge may hand you over to the officer, and you may be thrown into prison. I tell you the truth, you will not get out until you have paid the last cent.'

By saying 'settle matters quickly' Jesus is saying that while we are still alive we need to actively seek reconciliation, as it will be too late to repent when we have died.

Luke also covered this teaching of Jesus, that we all need to repent.

Luke 13:1: 'Now there were some present at that time who told Jesus about the Galileans whose blood Pilate had mixed with their sacrifices. Jesus answered, "Do you think that these Galileans were worse sinners than all the other Galileans because they suffered this way? I tell you, no! But unless you repent, you too will all perish. Or those eighteen who died when the tower in Siloam fell on them – do you think they were more guilty than all the others living in Jerusalem? I tell you, no! But unless you repent, you too will all perish."

Here Jesus is taking the people's thoughts away from headline-grabbing news events and bringing them back to reality and to their own lives. The message was 'forget about what's happening around you and concentrate on putting yourself right with God.'

This starts with repentance, which is not simply about saying sorry for previous sins, but it also means turning away from sin.

Our relationship with God has to start with us understanding what's expected of us and recognising the areas in which we have failed. We then need to repent by asking for forgiveness and by turning from those sins. As with an alcoholic or drug addict, the healing starts with an acknowledgement that there is a problem and so it is with our relationship with Jesus.

By working on our failings and expanding on the good things we're doing, we start walking on the path to salvation. Repentance is not a one-off event but rather something we should be doing on a regular basis, because we will still inevitably sin even though we have faith.

Matthew 13:13: 'This is why I speak to them in parables. 'Though seeing, they do not see; though hearing, they do not hear or understand. In them is fulfilled the prophecy of Isaiah: 'You will be ever hearing but never understanding; you will be ever seeing but never perceiving.

For this people's heart has become calloused; they hardly hear with their ears, and they have closed their eyes. Otherwise they might see with their eyes, hear with their ears, understand with their hearts and turn, and I would heal them.'

But blessed are your eyes because they see, and your ears because they hear. For I tell you the truth, many prophets and righteous men longed to see what you see but did not see it, and to hear what you hear but did not hear it.'

Again the word 'turn' is key-critical and Jesus promises that if we turn from our sins then he will swiftly offer His healing. It's a free gift but often pride prevents people from accessing this grace, as it's all too easy for us to rationalise away our sins and to see no reason why we should have to repent. In this situation our hearts will have become calloused because we have lost the sense of sin.

Luke 23:39: One of the criminals who hung there hurled insults at him: "Aren't you the Christ? Save yourself and us!"

But the other criminal rebuked him. "Don't you fear God," he said, "since you are under the same sentence? We are punished justly, for we are getting what our deeds deserve. But this man has done nothing wrong." Then he said, "Jesus, remember me when you come into your kingdom."

Jesus answered him, "I tell you the truth, today you will be with me in paradise."

Dismas, the good thief, repented at the very end of his life, analogous to someone repenting and accepting Jesus on their deathbed. To me Dismas made the perfect confession as he acknowledged his sins and that his condition had been self inflicted.

He also recognised the need for forgiveness and he joined his sufferings to that of Jesus hanging next to him. The perfection of his repentance and the fact that he had no further possibility to sin in his life as he was dying, meant that he could go straight to Heaven. This gives us all hope as it's never too late to repent and to turn to God and ask for healing.

-Chapter 12-

The sins of our modern world

As God's laws are immutable they need to be the benchmark by which our actions are deemed sinful or not. It's easy for us to forget that God's definition of what constitutes sin is timeless, unlike man's laws which constantly evolve and redefine what actions are legal and which are not. At no time in modern history has there been such a great gulf between the two and we now have protected in law actions which are clearly contrary to God's laws. Part of the reason why this has happened is the ascendency of individual liberty and a focus on protecting the rights of the individual, sometimes to the detriment of the wider society.

Jesus himself taught that God's laws were permanent.

Matthew 5:17: Do not think that I have come to abolish the Law or the Prophets; I have not come to abolish them but to fulfill them. I tell you the truth, until heaven and earth disappear, not the smallest letter, not the least stroke of a pen, will by any means disappear from the Law until everything is accomplished.

Luke 16:16: The Law and the Prophets were proclaimed until John. Since that time, the good news of the kingdom of God is being preached, and everyone is forcing their way into it. It is easier for heaven and earth to disappear than for the least stroke of a pen to drop out of the Law.

The commandments were a simple and effective way of giving laws to everyone regardless of their level of education and by implementing them society would remain in an orderly state. The second census of the Israelites wandering in the desert gave a population of 601,730 men over the age of twenty and in addition to this there were 23,000 male Levites aged one month and older. If we were to include women and those under the age of twenty, then we would surely have a figure of a few million Israelites!

To control this population that lacked the infrastructure and administration of a large city and that was often on the move, meant that a strict code of rules and observances had to be devised. So the

Ten Commandments were an ideal core of rules to ensure stability and cohesion in this nomadic society.

Subcategories to each commandment were added and ultimately there evolved rules for worship; for separating diseased persons from the community, for minor and major offences against the person, etc. The phrase 'an eye for an eye and a tooth for a tooth' originated in this period and was the overarching principle of restitution or of seeking damages.

The commandments set forth that love for God must be above all else and the first three commandments are centered on this theme – 'you shall have no other Gods before me,' 'you shall not misuse the name of the Lord your God' and 'observe the Sabbath day by keeping it holy.'

They protect the family in the commandments 'honour your father and your mother,' 'you shall not commit adultery' and 'you shall not steal.' They also protect marriage in the two commandments 'you shall not commit adultery' and 'you shall not covet your neighbour's wife.'

Finally the Decalogue protects the person in the commandments 'you shall not murder,' 'you shall not steal' and 'you shall not give false testimony.' This last commandment also helps to ensure integrity in the legal system.

Now if we judge our society against the Ten Commandments we see the perilous state of our World at this time. The first commandment is under threat through a tremendous rise in atheism in the World and Jesus himself cited the most serious of all sins being blasphemy against the Holy Spirit.

Matthew 12:30: 'He who is not with me is against me, and he who does not gather with me scatters. And so I tell you, every sin and blasphemy will be forgiven men, but the blasphemy against the Spirit will not be forgiven. Anyone who speaks a word against the Son of Man will be forgiven, but anyone who speaks against the Holy Spirit will not be forgiven, either in this age or in the age to come.'

Here Jesus is saying that there's no middle ground or grey area and that each individual has a choice to either reject him or to accept him. A conscious and final decision to reject God in ones' life, would deny that person access to the grace of salvation through the sacrifice of His Son on the cross. This passage also supports the teaching of the existence of Purgatory as clearly some sins are able to be forgiven in the life after death.

Luke 12:8: "I tell you, whoever acknowledges me before men, the Son of Man will also acknowledge him before the angels of God. But he who disowns me before men will be disowned before the angels of God."

John 3:16: "For God so loved the world that he gave his one and only Son, that whoever believes in him shall not perish but have eternal life. For God did not send his Son into the world to condemn the world, but to save the world through him. Whoever believes in him is not condemned, but whoever does not believe stands condemned already because he has not believed in the name of God's one and only Son."

Atheism is clearly a denial of God, His son Jesus and the Holy Spirit and here Jesus reminds us that this is the only sin which can never be forgiven. In our modern western societies atheism is at an all time high but there's also been a massive rise in the number of agnostics, people who say they believe in God but who don't practice their faith. The first commandment is also being undermined through rampant consumerism and God's name is profaned constantly on television and in general conversation.

The Sabbath is only kept holy by about 13% of the UK population which is the percentage who regularly attend church services. If we look at the command 'honour your father and your mother' we see that respect for the elderly is sadly lacking in our western culture.

Then if we take the commandment 'you shall not kill' we see abortion happening on an unprecedented scale in our society and active or passive euthanasia being practiced. Abortion was illegal in 1917 worldwide and was carried out on a miniscule scale compared to today. Pope John Paul II released the encyclical '**Evangelium Vitae**' on the **25th of March 1995** concerning the inviolability of human life and specifically covered murder, abortion and euthanasia.

There's often a double standard at play whereby in some countries abortion is legal and yet the death penalty is still sanctioned for murder. Why are rights only conferred on babies at birth? Surely just because a foetus is still within the environment of a mother's body, it shouldn't forfeit its right to protection from harm? Indeed the very morphology of the womb is designed to protect the foetus from harm.

The number of abortions being carried out is simply staggering and the Guttmacher Institute estimated that there were 43.8 million abortions in 2008 alone. The worldwide abortion rate in 2008 was 28 abortions per 1000 women of child bearing age (15 to 44 years), so this means that almost 3% of women of child bearing age had an abortion in that year.

When it comes to the number of abortions carried out in countries like China the numbers are difficult to comprehend. A report by the World Health Organisation and the Guttmacher Institute put the figure at 9 million per annum, but other sources have quoted a figure of at least 13 million each year. In China about two thirds of the women having an abortion are between the ages of twenty and twenty-nine and most are single women. This excludes abortions connected with the 10 million abortion pills sold annually!

In Russia there are about 2 million abortions each year and the abortion rate is extremely high as a percentage of the population, at 53.7 abortions per 1000 women. In other words 5.4% of women of child bearing age have an abortion in Russia each year. In China although overall numbers of abortions are very much higher, the abortion rate is about 24 per 1000 women.

In England and Wales alone in 2011 there were 196,082 abortions and in the US there were about 1.21 million abortions each year for the period 2008 to 2011. These are abortions registered with the authorities so the actual number will be far higher in these countries.

A few of the declarations from the Pope's encyclical were:

Evangelium Vitae 58: Among all the crimes which can be committed against life, procured abortion has characteristics making it particularly serious and deplorable. The Second Vatican Council defines abortion, together with infanticide, as an 'unspeakable crime.'

Evangelium Vitae 61: The texts of Sacred Scripture never address the question of deliberate abortion and so do not directly and specifically condemn it. But they show such great respect for the human being in the mother's womb that they require as a logical consequence that God's commandment "You shall not kill" be extended to the unborn child as well....Christian Tradition - as the Declaration issued by the Congregation for the Doctrine of the Faith points out so well -- is clear and unanimous, from the beginning up to our own day, in describing abortion as a particularly grave moral disorder.

Evangelium Vitae 62: Given such unanimity in the doctrinal and disciplinary tradition of the Church, Paul VI was able to declare that this tradition (regarding abortion) is unchanged and unchangeable. Therefore, by the authority which Christ conferred upon Peter and his Successors, in communion with the Bishops - who on various occasions have condemned abortion and who in the aforementioned consultation, albeit dispersed throughout the world, have shown unanimous agreement concerning this doctrine - I declare that direct abortion, that is, abortion willed as an end or as a means, always constitutes a grave moral disorder, since it is the deliberate killing of an innocent human being. This doctrine is based upon the natural law and upon the written Word of God, is transmitted by the Church's Tradition and taught by the ordinary and universal Magisterium.

The Pope was correct in his comments in EV61 that direct abortion is not specifically covered in the Bible. However I would argue that it is covered by implication, since the issue of the accidental harming or killing of an unborn child is specifically covered in **Exodus 21:22**:

"If men who are fighting hit a pregnant woman and she gives birth prematurely but there is no serious injury, the offender must be fined whatever the woman's husband demands and the court allows. But if there is serious injury, you are to take life for life, eye for eye, tooth for tooth, hand for hand, foot for foot, burn for burn, wound for wound, bruise for bruise."

So it's clear from this text that the protection of the unborn child was enshrined in Mosaic Law. It's also implicit that if the accidental killing of an unborn baby warranted the death penalty, then clearly the deliberate killing of an unborn baby would certainly have warranted it under Mosaic Law.

This view is echoed in the words of Tertullian in his work the Apologeticum written around 197 AD. Chapter 9 verse 8:

"In our case, a murder being once for all forbidden, we may not destroy even the fetus in the womb, while as yet the human being derives blood from the other parts of the body for its sustenance. To hinder a birth is merely a speedier man-killing; nor does it matter whether you take away a life that is born, or destroy one that is coming to birth. That is a man which is going to be one; you have the fruit already in its seed."

Other sins that have become far more prominent in modern times include pornography and paedophilia. Society immerses us in a diametrically opposed doctrine to that of Jesus and it constantly promotes the idea that we are sexual and not spiritual beings. It also exposes our young and vulnerable children to unprecedented levels of sex and violence in so called 'games' and movies.

And yet these children are precious to Jesus and it's his will that they should all be saved. In fact children are so close to God their creator, that the angels of these children see the very face of God, the beatific vision. The sexual abuse of children is clearly an affront to God and our society needs to heed the words of Jesus on the subject of children.

Matthew 18:10: See that you do not look down on one of these little ones. For I tell you that their angels in heaven always see the face of my Father in heaven.

Matthew 18:5: "And whoever welcomes a little child like this in my name welcomes me. But if anyone causes one of these little ones who believe in me to sin, it would be better for him to have a large millstone hung around his neck and to be drowned in the depths of the sea. Woe to the world because of the things that cause people to sin! Such things must come but woe to the man through whom they come!"

If we take the commandment, 'Thou shall not steal' we see the emergence of theft at the corporate level that has emerged in our recent history. It was the drive to maximise profits and bonuses that spurned the reckless mortgage lending and use of insurance derivatives, which caused the turmoil of the financial crisis that began in 2008. There's been a spectacular rise in wealth but our materialism has resulted in a huge disconnect between the wealthy and poor nations. The proliferation of sweat shops in the East to provide cheap clothing for rich western nations has resulted in very poor and dangerous working conditions and low pay for many workers. Even within Western societies there is now a very wide gulf between the rich and the poor.

Mary appeared at Fatima to warn us that our sins were greatly offending God and that there were consequences for this at both the individual and the global level. The carnage of World War II came about as a consequence of sin in our World, but it wasn't just the sinners who suffered the consequences of this 6 year war and many of the 85 million victims were innocent. So it's clear that Mary called all mankind to repent and to pray, not just for ourselves and our personal failings, but to mitigate the overall sinfulness in the World. Similarly her request for us to adopt the First Five Saturdays devotion is to make reparation for the sins committed against her by countless sinners.

At Fatima Our Lady implored us to repent, to stop sinning and to turn to prayer and she warned very graphically of the reality of Hell for unrepentant sinners. Some sins are clearly common to all ages but others have become very prominent in our modern World, such as atheism and rampant abortion.

So in respect of sin, is the World in a better state now than it was in 1917? It would seem that it's a few orders of magnitude worse! Our Lady told the children in 1917 that God was offended and outraged by the sins being committed then, but how much more is He being offended today? Surely there has never been a greater need for repentance and for turning to God in prayer.

In a radio message on the 26th of October 1946 to the U.S. National Catechetical Congress in Boston, Pope Pius XII said:

'The sin of the century is the loss of the sense of sin.'

These words were later quoted by John Paul II at the Synod of Bishops in October 1983, which was a month long synod convened to discuss 'Reconciliation and Penance in the Mission of the Church.' John Paul II reiterated that penance was closely connected with reconciliation to God. Regarding the vital role of Our Lady he said the following:

'The first means of this salvific action is that of prayer. It is certain that the Blessed Virgin, mother of Christ and of the church, and the saints, who have now reached the end of their earthly journey and possess God's glory, sustain by their intercession their brethren who are on pilgrimage through the world, in the commitment to conversion, to faith, to getting up again after every fall, to acting in order to help the growth of communion and peace in the church and in the world.'

-Chapter 13-
Purgatory

Our lady used the word 'Purgatory' at the first apparition on the 13th of May 1917 and it's interesting that the gospels record at least 28 references to Hell and 8 references to Purgatory made by Jesus, although the references to Purgatory are implied, as He didn't use that term. Apart from these there are numerous other references to Hell and to Purgatory in the New Testament such as in Paul and Peter's letters and in the Book of Revelation.

God is perfect and it's intuitive that evil could not exist in His presence and this is also clear from scriptures.

Habakkuk 1:13: 'Your eyes are too pure to look on evil; you cannot tolerate wrong.'

This is also evident from the account of the fall of man in Genesis, where Adam and Eve had to leave the Garden of Eden because they had sinned.

Again we can conclude this from what God said to Moses on Mount Sinai before He came down on the mountain:

Exodus 19:12: "Put limits for the people around the mountain and tell them, 'Be careful that you do not go up the mountain or touch the foot of it. Whoever touches the mountain shall surely be put to death.'"

So after death, a soul would not immediately be able to exist in Heaven with Almighty God without undergoing purification.

Now it's clear from 2 Maccabees that it was customary to offer sacrifice for the souls of the dead as far back as the second century BC.

2 Maccabees 12:43-46: 'And making a gathering, he sent twelve thousand drachmas of silver to Jerusalem for sacrifice to be offered for the sins of the dead, thinking well and religiously concerning the resurrection (For if he had not hoped that they that were slain should rise again, it would have seemed superfluous and vain to pray for the dead). And because he considered that they who had fallen asleep with godliness, had great grace laid up for them. It is therefore a holy and wholesome thought to pray for the dead, that they may be loosed from sins.'

The Maccabees were the leaders of a Jewish rebellion against the Seleucid Dynasty and books 1 and 2 outline some of their history from about 175 to 134 BC. The Seleucid Empire was a Hellenistic state formed under the command of Seleucus after the break up of the empire that had been created by Alexander the Great.

The Catholic Church definition of Purgatory is that 'it is a place or condition of temporal punishment for those who, departing this life in God's grace, are, not entirely free from venial faults, or who have not fully paid the satisfaction due to their transgressions.'

Augustine made a distinction between 'the temporal purifying fire of Purgatory that saves' and 'the eternal consuming fire for the unrepentant.' Thomas Aquinas also wrote that the souls in Purgatory are at peace, because they are assured of salvation and they are helped by the prayers of the faithful.

The doctrine on Purgatory was expressed in the Decree of Union drawn up by the Council of Florence in 1438, where the teaching on Purgatory was heavily debated. What's surprising is just how far back the practice of offering prayers and the Eucharist for the souls of the dead is found in historic writings.

For example it's described by one of the church fathers, Tertullian who was the son of a centurion and who converted to Christianity in Carthage in 192 AD. His interest in the religion of Christianity came about because he was 'staggered' by the constancy of Christians under brutal persecution. It's thought that Tertullian worked for a time as an advocate in the law courts before taking to writing.

Tertullian produced dozens of works including 'The Apologeticum' in which he described a report made by Pilate to the Emperor Tiberius that he had 'pronounced the unjust sentence of death against an innocent and divine person.' (Chapters 5 and 21).

Tertullian wrote in **De Anima**: Full well the soul will know in Hades how to feel joy or sorrow even without the body. The 'prison' of the Gospel (Matt. v. 25) was Hades, and 'the uttermost farthing' the very smallest offence which had to be atoned there before the resurrection. Hence the soul must undergo in Hades some compensatory discipline without prejudice to the full accomplishment of the resurrection, when recompense would be paid to the flesh also.

Tertullian also described the practice of praying for the dead in chapter 3 of **De Corona militis**, which he wrote around 211 AD :

'We take also, in congregations before daybreak, and from the hand of none but the presidents, the sacrament of the Eucharist, which the Lord both commanded to be eaten at meal-times, and enjoined to be taken by all alike. As often as the anniversary comes round, we make offerings for the dead as birthday honours.'

In chapter X of his work **De Monogamia** he wrote on the subject of marriage and the loss of a spouse:

'Indeed, she prays for his soul, and requests refreshment for him meanwhile, and fellowship (with him) in the first resurrection; and she offers (her sacrifice) on the anniversaries of his falling asleep.'

So it's clear that it's been a long-standing practice both among the Jews and later the Christians to pray for the souls of the dead and inherent in this is the belief that souls after death can receive benefit from the prayers and the Eucharist offered up for them. From Maccabees we can see that the prayers and sacrifices were offered to free the souls from their sins, so that they could participate in the resurrection of the dead.

This is a subject that Catholic priests seem reticent to tackle in their homilies today, which is a great pity. Failing to ever talk about Purgatory or Hell leads the faithful into a false sense of security and it also surely helps break the link with the need for confession.

I worry about the children attending mass every week who are growing up never hearing the subject of Purgatory covered in a single homily in their lives. Jesus spoke about Hell with alarming regularity and it's difficult to imagine that He would do anything else if He were on Earth today.

It was during the reformation that the reformers rejected the doctrine of Purgatory although it's interesting that there was hesitation by Martin Luther. But let's look at the words of Jesus himself which may relate to a punishment or purification of a soul after death.

Matthew 5:25: Settle matters quickly with your adversary who is taking you to court. Do it while you are still with him on the way, or he may hand you over to the judge, and the judge may hand you over to the officer, and you may be thrown into prison. I tell you the truth, you will not get out until you have paid the last cent.

Here we need to look at the context of this statement by Jesus. He was talking about the interpretation of the Law and warning the crowds about the implications of sinning and in verses 21 and 27 (i.e. before and after this statement) he spoke of the risk of sinners being sent to Hell. It's clear then that he wasn't talking about an earthly prison but a state of existence after death.

His words, 'you will not get out until you have paid the last cent' indicate that there is a debt or record of sin for which recompense must be made after we have died. He was saying that we have an opportunity while we are still alive to put things right and to avoid the punishment due for those offences.

We can confess our sins at any time to a priest and receive the grace of forgiveness in the sacrament of reconciliation, but we often hold back from doing this for a variety of reasons. It may be that we don't see the need to confess to a priest, because we just say sorry to God directly, as his sacrifice at Calvary nullifies our sins anyway.

However we need to remember that Jesus empowered his apostles to forgive sins **after** the resurrection. If he believed that post resurrection, it was no longer necessary for man to go through a priest to ask for forgiveness, then why did he empower them in this way after he had risen from the dead?

John 20:21: Again Jesus said, "Peace be with you! As the Father has sent me, I am sending you." And with that he breathed on them and said, "Receive the Holy Spirit. **If you forgive anyone his sins, they are forgiven; if you do not forgive them, they are not forgiven.**"

Another reason for putting off going to confession is pride and another may be that we have rationalised away our failings and no longer see them as sins anymore. It's helpful for us to remember that in Confession and in the celebration of the Eucharist, the priest is acting 'In Persona Christi,' a Latin phrase meaning 'In the Person of Christ.'

Also, confession is a sacrament in its own right and so each time we attend we will receive the graces of the Holy Spirit.

Mark 9:49: And if your eye causes you to sin, pluck it out. It is better for you to enter the kingdom of God with one eye than to have two eyes and be thrown into hell, where 'their worm does not die, and the fire is not quenched.' Everyone will be salted with fire.

If we look at the first part of this statement i.e. excluding 'Everyone will be salted with fire,' Jesus is talking about a permanent state which is Hell. The soul cannot be removed from this state because the condition of the soul is fixed at death and Jesus is saying that we have the opportunity now, while we are alive to do something about our sinfulness. He's saying that whatever short term gain or pleasure is derived from sins in our earthly life is just not worth the risk of losing our eternal happiness for them.

Perhaps this is part of the problem – that it's difficult for us to comprehend the magnitude of the joy that awaits us in Heaven and that this is for all eternity. It's much like considering the distance of stars from the Earth or the sheer scale of the universe.

This was possibly one reason that Jesus showed Peter, James and John the magnificence of the transfiguration. They saw for a very short time the transfigured Jesus ablaze in glory, with his face shining like the sun and this is the glory that awaits us at the resurrection.

1 Corinthians 15:42: So will it be with the resurrection of the dead. The body that is sown is perishable; it is raised imperishable; it is sown in dishonour, it is raised in glory; it is sown in weakness, it is raised in power; it is sown a natural body, it is raised a spiritual body.

Philippians 3:20: But our citizenship is in heaven. And we eagerly await a Saviour from there, the Lord Jesus Christ. Who, by the power that enables him to bring everything under his control, will transform our lowly bodies so that they will be like his glorious body.

Now for the statement '**Everyone will be salted with fire**.' Here Jesus seems to be referring to what we term Purgatory, a state where we are somehow cleansed before entering Heaven. No-one dies in a perfect state - we have all sinned and it's unlikely that any of us have fully repented for all our sins at the time of death. Now as nothing impure can exist with God, it seems logical that the soul must first undergo purification.

Salt is added to food to improve it and to help bring out its flavours and so when Jesus says that everyone will be salted with fire, the objective of this 'salting' is clearly to improve us and not to harm us.

Jesus used this terminology on another occasion when he said, 'If salt loses its saltiness, how can it be made salty again?' Although the context was different, there is a parallel in that we can be made salty again in Purgatory. After death the soul leaves the body and we will have our personal judgment by Jesus where our final state will be revealed.

Clearly none of us attains eternal life through our efforts alone, as this is by virtue of Christ dying for us, but this is not to say that we can sit back and do nothing and there are obligations placed on us. If we have believed in Jesus and lived according to his commands and repented of our sins, then we will be guaranteed eternal life in Heaven. However there's a problem – we died with many sins not having been fully repented for and perhaps worse, still with a propensity to commit them again. We had not mastered our weaknesses, if you like.

What the nature of the purifying fire is, who can tell, but we need to remember that souls experiencing this are in God' love and that it is being done to bring us to perfection so that we can exist with Him.

Saint Catherine of Genoa (1447 - 1510) had a vision of Purgatory which she described as a 'loving fire.' She wrote that the fire was to 'purge them of all the rust and stains of sin of which they have not rid themselves in this life.' Her 'Treatise on Purgatory' makes very interesting reading!

How long do we spend in Purgatory? Again we cannot know, but time in Purgatory is disjointed time i.e. not directly linked to earthly time. So we shouldn't assume that a soul we've been praying for has already achieved purification and stop praying for that person and we should really pray for them indefinitely.

We don't talk much about 'The communion of saints' anymore but it's a teaching that we can help those in Purgatory by our prayers and by offering up masses for them. Importantly, the souls in Heaven can also help us! These souls in Purgatory can no longer help themselves and they are reliant on the compassion of God, but also on our prayers. This is why we should pray for the departed and we should also encourage our children to get into this habit too.

Matthew 11:11: I tell you the truth: Among those born of women there has not risen anyone greater than John the Baptist; yet he who is least in the kingdom of heaven is greater than he.

If John the Baptist was the greatest man who had ever lived and yet the least in Heaven is greater than he is, it surely indicates that souls are brought to a more perfect state after death. Even John the Baptist would require some form of purification before entering Heaven.

Matthew 18:23: Therefore the kingdom of heaven is like a king who wanted to settle accounts with his servants. As he began the settlement, a man who owed him ten thousand talents was brought to him. Since he was not able to pay, the master ordered that he and his wife and his children and all that he had be sold to repay the debt. The servant fell on his knees before him. "Be patient with me," he begged, "and I will pay back everything." The servant's master took pity on him, cancelled the debt and let him go.

But when that servant went out, he found one of his fellow servants who owed him a hundred denarii. He grabbed him and began to choke him. "Pay back what you owe me!" he demanded. His fellow servant fell to his knees and begged him, "Be patient with me, and I will pay you back." But he refused. Instead, he went off and had the man thrown into prison until he could pay the debt.

When the other servants saw what had happened, they were greatly distressed and went and told their master everything that had happened. Then the master called the servant in. "You wicked servant," he said, "I cancelled all that debt of yours because you begged me to. Shouldn't you have had mercy on your fellow servant just as I had on you?" In anger his master turned him over to the jailers to be tortured, until he should pay back all he owed. This is how my heavenly Father will treat each of you unless you forgive your brother from your heart.

This is one of several statements by Jesus to the effect that our forgiveness will be determined by how forgiving we have been in our dealings with others. A talent was a unit of measurement and the

Roman talent was 32.3 Kg whereas the Babylonian talent was 30.3 Kg. When a Talent was used to measure metals it was usually for precious metals like silver and gold and the talent was formed as a massive ingot with a handle on top. A strong man could carry one in each hand for a very short distance as each weighed a bit more than a bag of builder's sand.

In terms of value a talent of silver would be the value of that weight of silver and so one talent weighed the equivalent of about 6,000 Denarii. A Denarius was a small Roman silver coin roughly equivalent to a day's wages for a farm worker. A talent would therefore be about 6,000 days wages or over 16 years work, bearing in mind that silver was far more valuable then than it is today.

So in the parable the man owed the king the equivalent of 60 million days wages which was clearly impossible to repay by his own efforts in his lifetime. Despite this the king cancelled the entire debt as an act of mercy. In the same way it is impossible for us to pay off the debt that is required to enter eternal glory by our own efforts. The glory of living in God's presence for eternity is incomprehensibly great and we each have a debt of sin that we cannot possibly repay. However God writes off our debt through the sacrifice of His son.

Instead of being grateful and showing mercy himself he sets about chasing down those who owed him money and he has a poor man who owed him the equivalent of a few hundred day's wages thrown into prison. The response of the king was to turn him over to the jailers to be tortured. Notice how Jesus doesn't say tortured forever but instead **'until he should pay back all he owed.'** Purgatory unlike Hell, is not an everlasting state and is transient but our soul cannot leave there until it is completely sanctified.

1 Corinthians 3:11: But each one should be careful how he builds. For no one can lay any foundation other than the one already laid, which is Jesus Christ. If any man builds on this foundation using gold, silver, costly stones, wood, hay or straw, his work will be shown for what it is, because the Day will bring it to light. It will be revealed with fire, and the fire will test the quality of each man's work. If what he has built survives, he will receive his reward. If it is burned up, he will suffer loss; he himself will be saved, but only as one escaping through the flames.

It's difficult to see how Paul could have been referring to anything other than Purgatory here. The lighter materials such as wood, hay and straw will be burnt away, leaving what is precious behind. Our sins which we failed to repent of and our imperfections and attachments to sin, will be burnt away in the spiritual fire of God's love. The fire is not permanent and does not destroy, hence we escape through the flames. So unlike Hell, Purgatory is a transient phase that our souls pass through and it's fully for the benefit of our souls and leads to an ever closer union with God.

Hebrews 12:22: But you have come to Mount Zion, to the heavenly Jerusalem, the city of the living God. You have come to thousands upon thousands of angels in joyful assembly, to the church of the firstborn, whose names are written in heaven. You have come to God, the judge of all men, to **the spirits of righteous men made perfect**, to Jesus the mediator of a new covenant, and to the sprinkled blood that speaks a better word than the blood of Abel.

The 'spirits of righteous men made perfect' clearly implies that after death our souls can be made perfect. This purification comes from the grace of God's love, but again souls are also helped greatly by the prayers said for them and by masses offered up for their intention.

So there are several readings in the New Testament and Maccabees that clearly reference what the Church calls Purgatory. As mentioned at the beginning of this chapter, Our Lady also spoke about Purgatory and even called it by name at her first appearance to the children on the 13th of May 1917.

If the Church was in error in the teaching of the existence of Purgatory why would she have done this? By repenting of our sins and by acting on the call to the devotion Our Lady called for, we can surely reduce the length of time we will need to spend in Purgatory before entering our heavenly inheritance.

-Chapter 14-
Hell

On her third appearance at Fatima on the 13th of July 1917, Our Lady gave the children a terrifying vision of Hell which Lucia described as follows:

'The rays of light seemed to penetrate the earth, and we saw, as it were a sea of fire. Plunged in this fire were demons and souls in human form, like transparent burning embers, all blackened or burnished bronze, floating about in the conflagration, now raised into the air by the flames that issued from within themselves together with great clouds of smoke, now falling back on every side like sparks in huge fires, without weight or equilibrium, amid shrieks and groans of pain and despair, which horrified us and made us tremble with fear. The demons could be distinguished by their terrifying and repellent likeness to frightful and unknown animals, black and transparent like burning coals.'

Terrified and as if to plead for succour, we looked up at Our Lady, who said to us, so kindly and so sadly:

'You have seen Hell where the souls of poor sinners go. To save them, God wishes to establish in the world devotion to my Immaculate Heart. If what I say to you is done, many souls will be saved and there will be peace...'

So Our Lady linked the devotion to her Immaculate Heart that she asked for, to the salvation of souls and also to peace in the World. Her appearances at Fatima were quite clearly out of concern for the souls who were in danger of going to Hell if they didn't repent and turn from their sins.

During his three year public ministry Jesus was also at pains to warn us of the reality of Hell and there are about 28 references to it in the gospels. This includes situations where Jesus described Hell without using that term, but where he alluded to it with phrases like 'weeping and gnashing of teeth' or 'where their worm does not die' or 'where the fire does not go out,' etc.

This state of existence that Jesus warned us about on so many occasions is almost never mentioned in our modern World and seems to have drifted into the realm of folklore and legend. However the Church teaching is that a person dying in a state of 'mortal' sin would be unable to enter Heaven and would exist in the state we know as Hell for all eternity. This is why it is so important for us to repent of our sins on a regular basis and the grace of forgiveness is always available in the confessional. From the teachings of Jesus we know that Hell is undoubtedly a place of suffering, that it is a place for souls who have died out of God's love and that it is a permanent existence.

Matthew 5:21: 'You have heard that it was said to the people long ago, 'Do not murder, and anyone who murders will be subject to judgment.' But I tell you that anyone who is angry with his brother will be subject to judgment. Again, anyone who says to his brother, 'Raca,' is answerable to the Sanhedrin. But anyone who says, 'You fool!' will be in danger of the fire of Hell. Therefore, if you are offering your gift at the altar and there remember that your brother has something against you, leave the gift there in front of the altar. First go and be reconciled to your brother; then come and offer your gift.'

There's some controversy over the meaning of the word 'raca' as although it is present in the Greek manuscripts it is not a Greek word. It's possibly referring to the Aramaic word reka meaning empty one or probably empty headed or foolish. In Greek the word fool is translated as moros which usually has a similar meaning to reka but moros can also mean godless, which would be more insulting. So either way it was definitely a word used as an insult. Jesus used the word himself to criticise the Pharisees in Matthew 23:17 calling them 'You blind fools!'

Here Jesus is taking the commandments to another level – a quantum shift in interpretation. He is showing that it is not just a contravention of the commandments that could result in us going to Hell but also sins which seem less significant. God wants sincere worship and it would be hypocritical of us to hold angry feelings in our hearts and yet to offer up prayers in church. We surely need reconciliation first.

Although Jesus went to great lengths to warn us of the existence of Hell, priests no longer seem to ever cover it in their homilies. I wonder if this is out of fear of upsetting the congregations or perhaps it's some form of religious political correctness. There has been a dramatic change in other areas of life in the last generation such as discipline in the home and in the school, where the pendulum has swung through 180 degrees. In the Church I suspect the feeling is that they had placed too much emphasis on Hell and Purgatory in the past and so they too have swung through 180 degrees. But is the balance right now? Perhaps we should ask ourselves: 'If Jesus returned to Earth now, would he be discussing Hell on a regular basis or not?'

Yes the very nature of God is about love, mercy and forgiveness and it's obviously right that this aspect is emphasised in homilies. However, God is also about justice and unrepented sins will not go unpunished and so it's critical that priests get the balance right.

One of the gifts of the Holy Spirit is 'fear of the Lord' and for good reason, as fear of punishment helps us to avoid sin. If priests no longer explain this teaching of the Church then who will do it? Is it then just up to parents to do so?

It's evident from scripture that God's plan for mankind encompasses order and justice. Hence for example the sanctity of marriage and therefore the family unit, is protected under the commandment 'thou shall not commit adultery.' Similarly property is protected under 'thou shall not steal', etc. It's natural therefore for Purgatory and Hell to exist because if there was no punishment for misdeeds in this World then chaos and disorder would surely rule.

A frequently asked question is 'How could a loving God create a state like Hell'? But perhaps the question is misguided and part of the answer is found in **Revelation 12:7**:

'And war broke out in heaven: Michael and his angels fought with the dragon; and the dragon and his angels fought, but they did not prevail, nor was a place found for them in heaven any longer. So the great dragon was cast out, that serpent of old, called the Devil and Satan, who deceives the whole world; he was cast to the earth, and his angels were cast out with him.'

Revelation 12:3: 'And another sign appeared in heaven: behold, a great, fiery red dragon having seven heads and ten horns, and seven diadems on his heads. His tail drew a third of the stars of heaven and threw them to the earth.'

So the revolt against God resulted in one third of the angels being banished from Heaven and from then on there existed a state outside of Heaven that was under the control of Satan and his angels. Souls existing in this environment are unprotected by God's love and will remain in a permanent state of separation from that love. This in effect is Hell – a state of permanent separation from the love of God.

So we shouldn't blame God for sending souls to Hell. Rather, an individual who chooses to reject God in his life, either by denying his existence or by living a sinful life and dying in an unrepentant state, has placed himself in this realm.

Matthew 5:27: You have heard that it was said, "Do not commit adultery." But I tell you that anyone who looks at a woman lustfully has already committed adultery with her in his heart. If your right eye causes you to sin, gouge it out and throw it away. It is better for you to lose one part of your body than for your whole body to be thrown into hell. And if your right hand causes you to sin, cut it off and throw it away. It is better for you to lose one part of your body than for your whole body to go into hell.

Here Jesus is again asking us to go beyond the commandment 'Thou shall not commit adultery' and to go to the precursors of that sin. The sin of adultery doesn't just happen and it begins long before the sexual act itself. Jesus is also showing that serious sin has an eternal consequence and that we must stop at nothing to protect our souls. Surely eternal life in Heaven is the greatest of treasures and the one that we must do everything to safeguard.

Mark 9:47: And if your eye causes you to sin, pluck it out. It is better for you to enter the kingdom of God with one eye than to have two eyes and be thrown into hell, where 'their worm does not die, and the fire is not quenched.'

From this and many other statements by Jesus it's clear that a soul in Hell is there permanently and this links in with what Saint Paul wrote on the subject.

2 Thessalonians 1:8: 'He will punish those who do not know God and do not obey the gospel of our Lord Jesus. They will be punished with everlasting destruction and shut out from the presence of the Lord and from the majesty of his power.'

Jesus often mentioned fire when describing Hell and this was also evident in the vision that Our Lady gave to the children at Fatima and many of the saints have had similar visions.

Sister Maria Faustina Kowalska (1905-1938) is regarded as being one of the most distinguished mystics in the history of the Church. At nineteen she entered the Congregation of Our Blessed Lady of Mercy in Warsaw as Elena Kowalska. Sister Faustina was given visions of both Purgatory and Hell and she described the fire in Hell as 'the fire that will penetrate the soul without destroying it. A terrible suffering since it is a purely spiritual fire, lit by God's anger.'

She was also given a vision of Jesus in which he asked her to paint him as he had appeared and for her to put the words, 'Jesus, I trust in you!' at the bottom of the painting. Jesus also asked her to have the first Sunday after Easter designated the Feast of the Divine Mercy.

On another visit on the 13th of September 1935, while she was in Vilnius, Jesus gave her the prayers which we know as the '**Chaplet of Divine Mercy**.' Sister Faustina saw an apparition of an angel who was about to punish the World, but the words of the chaplet were then given to her and when she recited them she saw that the punishment that was to afflict the Earth was pushed away. The next day Jesus appeared to her once more and again gave the words of the chaplet and explained how they should be prayed.

The chaplet begins with one Our Father, one Hail Mary and then the Apostle's creed. On the beads of the Our Father one should say:

'Eternal Father, I offer You the Body, Blood, Soul and Divinity of your dearly beloved Son, Our Lord Jesus Christ, in atonement for our sins and those of the whole world.'

On the Hail Mary beads one should say: 'For the sake of His sorrowful passion have mercy on us and on the whole world.'

At the end of the five decades Our Lord said that we should say three times: 'Holy God, Holy Mighty One, Holy Immortal One, have mercy on us and on the whole world.'

During subsequent apparitions to Sister Faustina, Jesus gave the assurance that people who recited the chaplet **would be given the grace of a happy and peaceful death**. He also said to Sister Faustina that people reciting the chaplet could ask God for everything that was concordant with His will. Jesus also urged people to recite this chaplet in the presence of those who were dying and he said:

"I desire to give inconceivable graces to souls who trust My mercy."

In 1936 Jesus again appeared to Sister Faustina when she was in Warsaw and he gave her the 'Hour of Mercy' prayer. This prayer is to be said at 3 o'clock each day, the time of the death of Jesus and the moment at which his sacrifice on the cross opened up a fountain of mercy for the World. He said that in this moment, mercy is opened broadly for every soul. The prayers are:

"You expired Jesus but the source of life gushed forth for souls and the ocean of Mercy opened up for the whole World. O Fount of Life, unfathomable Divine Mercy, envelop the whole World and empty Yourself out upon us.'

'O Blood and Water which gushed forth from the Heart of Jesus as a Fount of Mercy for us, I trust in You.'

Sister Faustina died of tuberculosis in her convent on the 5th of October 1938. On the 18th of April 1993, the first Sunday after Easter, John Paul II beatified Sister Faustina and on the 30th of April 2000 he canonized her. The pope also declared that the first Sunday after Easter would be the Feast of Divine Mercy.

So the fire of Hell that Sister Faustina saw in her vision, which in some ways resembles the appearance of physical fire but doesn't combust material immersed in it, is reminiscent of what Moses witnessed with the burning bush.

Exodus 3:2: There the angel of the Lord appeared to him in flames of fire from within a bush. Moses saw that though the bush was on fire it did not burn up.

In his gospel Luke gives an account of Jesus being asked the question, how many people will be saved.

Luke 13:22: Then Jesus went through the towns and villages, teaching as he made his way to Jerusalem. Someone asked him, "Lord, are only a few people going to be saved?"

He said to them, "Make every effort to enter through the narrow door, because many, I tell you, will try to enter and will not be able to. Once the owner of the house gets up and closes the door, you will stand outside knocking and pleading, 'Sir, open the door for us.' But he will answer, 'I don't know you or where you come from.'

Then you will say, 'We ate and drank with you, and you taught in our streets.' But he will reply, 'I don't know you or where you come from. Away from me, all you evildoers!'

There will be weeping there, and gnashing of teeth when you see Abraham, Isaac and Jacob and all the prophets in the kingdom of God, but you yourselves thrown out: People will come from east and west and north and south, and will take their places at the feast in the kingdom of God. Indeed there are those who are last who will be first, and first who will be last."

In Matthew's gospel there's also a passage where Jesus indicates that a large number of people will unfortunately go to Hell.

Matthew 7:13: Enter through the narrow gate. For wide is the gate and broad is the road that leads to destruction, and many enter through it. But small is the gate and narrow the road that leads to life, and only a few find it.

There's been debate about whether or not a narrow gate existed in the wall of Jerusalem named 'the eye of the needle' and it's possible that this was an inner gate and not one of the main gates of the city. The gate was apparently so narrow that traders would have to offload their goods and then lead the camel through the gate and the analogy is that we need to let go of physical attachments before we can enter Heaven. Whether or not this gate existed, Jesus makes it clear that the easy path in life will lead to Hell but the narrow and difficult road in life is the one that leads to eternal life.

Jesus also gave a warning to believers in him saying that not all believers would be saved either. Faith is essential but it must be accompanied by us living out our Christian lives in accordance with God's will. We need a holistic approach and so we can't 'cherry pick' the parts of Christian teaching that are easy for us to adopt and fail to live out the more difficult aspects of it.

Matthew 7:21: "Not everyone who says to me 'Lord, Lord' will enter the kingdom of heaven, but only he who does the will of my Father who is in heaven."

Matthew 10:28: 'Do not be afraid of those who kill the body but cannot kill the soul. Rather be afraid of the One who can destroy both body and soul in hell.'

Here Jesus is telling us that in dictating our actions we need to see beyond the physical and to have in mind the protection of our souls which live for eternity. Our soul is by far our most precious asset! In this sense we must fear God, because although God is ever-loving He is also a God of justice.

Matthew 13:47: Once again, the kingdom of heaven is like a net that was let down into the lake and caught all kinds of fish. When it was full, the fishermen pulled it up on the shore. Then they sat down and collected the good fish in baskets, but threw the bad away. This is how it will be at the end of the age. The angels will come and separate the wicked from the righteous and throw them into the fiery furnace, where there will be weeping and gnashing of teeth. "Have you understood all these things?" Jesus asked.

Jesus here is using an analogy of catching fish, which he knew the uneducated people could relate to. The role that angels will perform at the end of time is explained and Hell is once again described as a fiery furnace. Jesus is at pains to get the message through because it's so fundamentally important, hence asking them, 'Have you understood all these things?'

Perhaps the most detailed description of Hell given by Jesus was in his parable of the rich man and Lazarus.

Luke 16:19: There was a rich man who was dressed in purple and fine linen and lived in luxury every day. At his gate was laid a beggar named Lazarus, covered with sores and longing to eat what fell from the rich man's table. Even the dogs came and licked his sores. The time came when the beggar died and the angels carried him to Abraham's side. The rich man also died and was buried.

In hell, where he was in torment, he looked up and saw Abraham far away, with Lazarus by his side. So he called to him, "Father Abraham, have pity on me and send Lazarus to dip the tip of his finger in water and cool my tongue, because I am in agony in this fire."

But Abraham replied, "Son, remember that in your lifetime you received your good things, while Lazarus received bad things, but now he is comforted here and you are in agony. And besides all this, between us and you a great chasm has been fixed, so that those who want to go from here to you cannot, nor can anyone cross over from there to us."

He answered, "Then I beg you, father, send Lazarus to my father's house, for I have five brothers. Let him warn them, so that they will not also come to this place of torment."

Abraham replied, "They have Moses and the Prophets; let them listen to them."

"No, father Abraham," he said, "but if someone from the dead goes to them, they will repent."

He said to him, "If they do not listen to Moses and the Prophets, they will not be convinced even if someone rises from the dead."

The crippled beggar in this parable was carried to the gate of the rich man in the hope of receiving food or money. Now his friends who carried him there wouldn't have done so if the rich man had a reputation for being cruel and this is the frightening facet of the story – that the rich man may have been a good man in some ways. This is evident in that while he was suffering in Hell, his thoughts were also on helping other people, not just on himself. So which commandment had he broken that condemned him to Hell?

Looking at a superficial level we could argue that he had broken none of them and that he was purely guilty of being negligent of the suffering around him. However looking deeper we could argue that he had broken the commandment 'Thou shall not steal' in a more general sense – stealing from the underprivileged in society. God puts wealth in the hands of certain people and it's an asset to be used for good purposes. Lavishing all that wealth on oneself is contrary to God's will as it maintains a gross inequality in society.

The rich man couldn't say that he was unaware of the man's plight because he was right at his gate and he would have seen him each time he entered and left the house. Indeed he even knew the beggar's name was Lazarus! He was probably embarrassed seeing the beggar there and wanted rid of him, but for some reason he didn't chase him away.

His attitude was probably one of, 'I've worked hard all my life to get to where I am; it's not my problem. Why don't his family help him?' It's also easy for us to assume the default position of saying, 'why don't they just get a job?' or 'why doesn't the State do something about it'?

Each beggar we see was once a young child in a class photograph. There was potential there, as in all the others in the photo but circumstances, probably including making poor choices in life, resulted in the person being where they are now. We shouldn't judge nor view them using the reference point of where we are in our own life and how we got to where we are now. The rich man passed Lazarus every day and probably avoided eye contact with him, as we may sometimes so ourselves when passing a beggar sitting on the ground with his blanket, his tin can and his dog.

And so it would appear from this parable that we can be sent to Hell for more subtle reasons than the overt breaking of commandments. In the case of the rich man his sin was that he had ignored the plight of those suffering around him when he was in a position to help.

Hell is again described as a place of agony and it's interesting that those in Hell are somehow aware of the joys of those in Heaven. The rich man in Hell had become fully aware of the need for repentance, but it was too late as he had been judged and his state was fixed for all eternity.

So his thoughts were on getting his family to repent and he asked Abraham to 'send' Lazarus to his father's house. The tone of this indicates another problem that the rich man had, as despite him being in Hell he still viewed Lazarus as somehow inferior; he was still like a servant to be bossed around. So in his lifetime the rich man was presumably bigoted and class conscious. The great chasm that Jesus described is interesting and shows that it's impossible for a soul to ever move from the one state to the other.

Matthew 25:1: "At that time the kingdom of heaven will be like ten virgins who took their lamps and went out to meet the bridegroom. Five of them were foolish and five were wise. The foolish ones took their lamps but did not take any oil with them. The wise ones, however, took oil in jars along with their lamps. The bridegroom was a long time in coming, and they all became drowsy and fell asleep. At midnight the cry rang out: 'Here's the bridegroom! Come out to meet him!' Then all the virgins woke up and trimmed their lamps.

The foolish ones said to the wise, 'Give us some of your oil; our lamps are going out.' 'No,' they replied, 'there may not be enough for both us and you. Instead, go to those who sell oil and buy some for yourselves.' But while they were on their way to buy the oil, the bridegroom arrived. The virgins who were ready went in with him to the wedding banquet. And the door was shut. Later the others also came. 'Lord, Lord,' they said, 'open the door for us!' But he replied, 'Truly I tell you, I don't know you.' Therefore keep watch, because you do not know the day or the hour."

Here Jesus is saying that we need to live our lives in a state of grace, prepared at any time to be called to give an account of ourselves. The five virgins who had no oil were not bad people as after all, they were invited to the wedding and they had arrived on time. But they were unprepared and focused on the wrong things. They were probably more concerned about how they looked as they were getting ready, than giving thought to what was required of them to carry out their duty. It's also all too easy for us to get caught up in our material lives and to put off till a later date the development of our relationship with God.

The parable reminds us that we need to think through what's required of us as Christians and this has parallels to the stories Jesus told of the man who intended to build a tower and of the king who intended with 10,000 men to fight another king with 20,000 men. Jesus said that surely they would have to think through what was required in advance. What's disconcerting is that the five virgins were not deemed fit for Heaven even though they had done many things right. In the same way the rich ruler who approached Jesus and asked what he must do to inherit eternal life had never broken a commandment and yet was deemed unworthy.

Matthew 25:41: Then he will say to those on his left, "Depart from me, you who are cursed, into the eternal fire prepared for the devil and his angels. For I was hungry and you gave me nothing to eat, I was thirsty and you gave me nothing to drink, I was a stranger and you did not invite me in, I needed clothes and you did not clothe me, I was sick and in prison and you did not look after me."

They also will answer, "Lord, when did we see you hungry or thirsty or a stranger or needing clothes or sick or in prison, and did not help you?"

He will reply, "Truly I tell you, whatever you did not do for one of the least of these, you did not do for me." Then they will go away to eternal punishment, but the righteous to eternal life.

Again Jesus is at pains to explain that we can be sent to Hell for being negligent of those in need around us. He focused on three areas – how we give to the poor, how we treat strangers and the visiting of the sick or those in prison. Mercy and love are at the heart of God and as Christians we are expected to show love to those in need. The parable of the Good Samaritan shows us true Christian love and how to be proactive in these areas. Showing love to the sick and to the needy have always been part of God's plan for His people.

Deuteronomy 10:18: 'He defends the cause of the fatherless and the widow, and loves the alien (stranger), giving him food and clothing. And you are to love those who are aliens, for you yourselves were aliens in Egypt.'

So at Fatima in 1917 Our Lady gave the children a terrifying vision of Hell and this has been passed on to us through the Church. It was clearly done to show us the reality of this permanent state of existence out of God's love and it was done out of concern for us by Our Blessed Mother. Mary gave us the First Five Saturday's devotion to help us as individuals, but also to help save souls from going to Hell.

-Chapter 15-
The great promise

When Our Lady appeared to the children for the second time on the 13th of June 1917 she said to Lucia:

"Jesus wishes to make use of you to make me known and loved. He wants to establish in the world devotion to my Immaculate Heart. I promise salvation to those who embrace it, and those souls will be loved by God like flowers placed by me to adorn his throne."

This was the first time that the request for this devotion had been mentioned by Our Lady and Lucia also described having seen something else during this encounter:

"In front of the palm of Our Lady's right hand was a Heart encircled by thorns which pierced it. We understood that this was the Immaculate Heart of Mary, outraged by the sins of humanity, and seeking reparation."

On her third visit Our Lady said, "Sacrifice yourself for sinners, and say many times, especially when you make some sacrifice: 'O Jesus, it is for love of You, for the conversion of sinners, and in reparation for sins committed against the Immaculate Heart of Mary.'"

So again the need for reparation was expressed by the Blessed Virgin.

After having shown them the vision of Hell Our Lady said:

'You have seen hell where the souls of poor sinners go. **To save them, God wishes to establish in the world devotion to my Immaculate Heart**. If what I say to you is done, many souls will be saved and there will be peace. The war is going to end; but if people do not cease offending God, a worse one will break out during the pontificate of Pius XI. When you see a night illumined by an unknown light, know that this is the great sign given you by God that He is about to punish the world for its crimes, by means of war, famine and persecutions of the Church and of the Holy Father. To prevent this, I shall come to ask for the consecration of Russia to my Immaculate Heart, and the Communion of Reparation on the First Saturdays. If my requests are heeded, Russia will be converted, and there will be peace; if not, she will spread her errors throughout the world, causing wars and persecutions of the Church. The good will be martyred, the Holy Father will have much to suffer, various nations will be annihilated. In the end, my Immaculate Heart will triumph. The Holy Father will consecrate Russia to me, and she will be converted, and a period of peace will be granted to the world. In Portugal, the dogma of the faith will always be preserved .."'

So here she said that it was God who wished to establish this devotion to her Immaculate Heart and it was for the first time that she used the term 'Communion of Reparation on the First Saturdays.'

When Lucia was in her room at the Dorothean convent on the 10th of December 1925, Our Lady again appeared to her with the child Jesus. She showed Lucia a heart encircled by thorns which she held in her hand and Jesus said:

"Have compassion on the Heart of your Most Holy Mother, covered with thorns, with which ungrateful men pierce it at every moment, and there is no one to make an act of reparation to remove them."

Our Lady then said, "Look, my daughter, at my Heart, surrounded with thorns with which ungrateful men pierce me at every moment by their blasphemies and ingratitude. You can at least try to console me and say that I promise to assist at the hour of death, with the graces necessary for salvation, all those who, for five consecutive months, shall confess, receive Holy Communion, recite five decades of the Rosary, and keep me company for fifteen minutes while meditating on the fifteen mysteries of the Rosary, with the intention of making reparation to me."

So here we have the specific details of how to make the devotion of the Communion of Reparation on the First Five Saturdays:

* Attend confession

* Receive Holy Communion

* Recite 5 decades of the Rosary

* Spend 15 minutes meditating on the 15 mysteries of the Rosary

The 15 minutes spent meditating is in addition to the reciting of the 5 decades of the Rosary and with all four elements of the devotion there has to be the intention of making reparation for the sins committed against the Immaculate Heart of Mary. The devotion has to be carried out on five consecutive first Saturdays of the month.

It's clear from the words used to describe the effect that these sins have on Our Lady that they are a source of very great hurt to her and also that there's little respite from that pain. The thorns of ungrateful men pierce it at every moment. Yes, at every moment! So the devotion she and her son Jesus asked for, give Our Lady consolation and remove the thorns from her heart.

Jesus again appeared to Lucia two months later in the convent garden at Pontevedra on the 15th of February 1926 and He spoke of this devotion:

"It is true, My daughter, that many souls begin, but few persevere to the very end, and those who persevere do it to receive the graces promised. The souls who make the five first Saturdays with fervor and to make reparation to the Heart of your Heavenly Mother, please Me more than those who make fifteen, but are lukewarm and indifferent."

Lucia then asked if it was possible to have a dispensation for people who found it difficult to attend confession on the Saturday.

She said, "My Jesus! Many souls find it difficult to confess on Saturday. Will You allow a confession within eight days to be valid?"

To this Jesus replied: "Yes. It can even be made later on, provided that the souls are in the state of grace when they receive Me on the first Saturday, and that they had the intention of making reparation to the Sacred Heart of Mary."

Lucia then asked, 'My Jesus! And those who forget to form this intention?'

Jesus replied, 'They can form it at the next confession, taking advantage of their first opportunity to go to confession.' After that the Child Jesus disappeared without saying anything more."

It's clear that the intention formed in this devotion is key critical and that it is in reparation for the sins against Mary. The promise she made is incredible, as she will assist at the hour of death all those who made the devotion with the graces necessary for their salvation.

Here is a very brief description of the mysteries of the Rosary and included are the Mysteries of Light, the Luminous mysteries, which John Paul II announced in 2002 and which cover a few of the key events in his three year public ministry.

Joyful Mysteries

The Annunciation: The angel Gabriel appeared to Mary saying, "Greetings you who are highly favoured! The Lord is with you." He then announced that Mary would conceive through the Holy Spirit and carry the Son of God in her womb and he also revealed that her cousin Elizabeth was herself six months pregnant.

The Visitation: Mary went to stay with Elizabeth for about three months, so up to about the time when Elizabeth gave birth to John the Baptist. The child in Elizabeth's womb jumped for joy at hearing Mary's voice and Elizabeth said, "Blessed are you among women, and blessed is the child you will bear!" So between Gabriel's greeting and the greeting of Elizabeth we have the first part of the prayer, The Hail Mary. Our Lady then sang a song in praise of God which we know as The Magnificat.

The Nativity: Joseph and Mary travelled from Nazareth in Galilee to Bethlehem in Judea, under very difficult conditions. This was to comply with the decree of Caesar Augustus that everyone had to travel to his home town to register for a population census. Mary gave birth under extremely poor circumstances but was visited by three practitioners of the monotheistic religion of Zoroastrianism.

They brought gold to signify the divinity and kingship of Jesus and frankincense, the fragrant white resin which was burned as an offering to God and which signified the holiness of the child Jesus. They also gave Myrrh, a spice derived from the resin of the low growing Myrrh tree, which was used in the embalming process. This gift was symbolic of suffering and was prophetic, as Jesus was offered the anaesthetising Myrrh mixed with wine at his crucifixion, but he refused to drink it. Joseph of Arimathea and Nicodemus would later use Myrrh and Aloes to embalm the body of Jesus.

The Presentation: On the eighth day Joseph and Mary took Jesus to the Temple in Jerusalem to be circumcised, as required by Mosaic Law and were met by Simeon in the Temple Courts. It had been revealed to Simeon by the Holy Spirit that he would not die until he had seen the Christ of God. Simeon praised and blessed Mary and Joseph, but he also cautioned Mary that a sword would pierce her own soul.

Finding in the Temple: Mary, Joseph and the twelve year old Jesus went up to Jerusalem for the annual celebration of the Passover but unknown to his parents, Jesus didn't join the caravan going back to Nazareth. They anxiously searched for him but only found Jesus three days later in the temple at Jerusalem, sitting with the teachers of The Law.

Luke 2:48: When his parents saw him, they were astonished. His mother said to him, "Son, why have you treated us like this? Your father and I have been anxiously searching for you." "Why were you searching for me?" he asked. "Didn't you know I had to be in my Father's house?"

Sorrowful mysteries

The agony in the garden: After the last supper Jesus crossed the Kidron valley with his disciples and walked to an olive grove called Gethsemane to pray. After a while he went a little farther into the olive grove with Peter, James and John and here he made the great act of faith that we can all imitate in times of great difficulty:

'Father, if you are willing, take this cup from me; yet not my will, but yours be done.'

His sweat looked like blood as it fell to the ground according to Luke, who was himself a physician. This is rare but happens under conditions of great stress, when the capillaries around the sweat glands constrict and later dilate to the extent that blood enters the sweat glands. Judas Iscariot arrived with the chief priests and the Temple Guard and betrayed Jesus with a kiss. Peter struck Malchus, the servant of the High Priest with his sword and cut off his right ear and then Jesus performed his last miracle by healing him.

The scourging at the pillar: Unlike the Jewish flogging of 40 lashes which traditionally ended at 39, the Roman scourging was very brutal and had no limit. It was called a half death and was designed to bring the victim close to death so that they would spend less time hanging on the cross. Before his trial by Pilate, Jesus had been beaten by the Jews after his trial before the Sanhedrin, at the house of Caiaphas. He was also beaten by the company of soldiers at the Praetorium, the official residence of the Roman Governor in Jerusalem.

The crowning with thorns: The same soldiers who had beaten Jesus then twisted some thorns into a crown and put it on his head. Then they dressed him in a scarlet robe and put a staff in his right hand, before kneeling down to mock him. Then they beat him over and over again with the staff on his head, according to Matthew's gospel account.

Carrying of the cross: Jesus was then led from the Praetorium carrying either the full cross or the beam of the cross, the Patibulum. The full cross is estimated to have weighed 135 Kg and the beam would have weighed about 45 Kg. Jesus was so weakened that he stumbled and fell for the first time and tradition tells us that it is then that he met his beloved mother. Jesus fell on another two occasions according to tradition and the guards forced a man named Simon from Cyrene to carry the cross or to help carry it on the Via Dolorosa. Simon is believed to have been a member of the large Jewish community who lived in Cyrene in Libya and was probably visiting Jerusalem for the feast, with his sons Alexander and Rufus. Jesus also met several of the women who had helped him on his three year ministry and he turned and said to them, "Daughters of Jerusalem, do not weep for me; weep for yourselves and for your children."

The crucifixion: Jesus was nailed to the cross by the four guards and hung between the two thieves Dismas and Gestas. Pilate had a notice pinned to the cross which read 'King of the Jews,' much to the anger of the chief priests. He hung on the cross for three hours when darkness mysteriously covered the land for a further three hours.

In his 'History of the Olympiads,' Phlegon wrote that it was so dark that the stars were plainly visible and it was also described by Tertullian in his work, 'The Apologeticum.' This darkness is inexplicable to scientists because it couldn't have been caused by a total solar eclipse as these can only happen at the time of a new moon and Passover is always celebrated at the time of a full moon! Besides this, the longest time a solar eclipse can ever last is 7 minutes and 31 seconds.

The soldiers cast lots for his undergarment as prophesied by David in Psalm 22, written a thousand years earlier. Gestas mocked Jesus but is rebuked by Dismas who then turned to Jesus and said, "Jesus remember me when you come into your kingdom."

Jesus replied, "I assure you, this very day you will be with me in paradise."

This confession by Dismas and the mercy and forgiveness he received show that it's never too late to repent.

Jesus uttered the words, "Eloi, Eloi, Lama Sabachthani?" meaning "My God, My God, why have you forsaken me?"

However this was not a cry of despair but the start of the wonderful Psalm 22 written by King David, which prophesied the crucifixion and the second part of the Psalm is all about praise of God.

Jesus saw his beloved mother standing there and gave his disciple John into her care and gave his mother to John. Jesus then said, "It is accomplished" and he died after having hung for six hours on the cross at Calvary.

Immediately there was a major earthquake, which was also described by Phlegon and for which there is also geological evidence. The great curtain in the Temple of Jerusalem, which was over 60 feet high and four inches thick, was torn in half, exposing the Holy of Holies. This section of the temple was reserved for the High Priest and he would walk through the curtain into the Holy of Holies to offer sacrifice for man's sins.

Now that Jesus had died for the sins of Mankind, he himself had become the sacrifice for sin. The crowds who had been mocking Jesus walked away beating their chests and the centurion Longinus standing at the cross said, "Surely this man was the Son of God!"

Glorious mysteries

The resurrection: The tomb was found empty on the Sunday morning by Mary Magdalene, Mary the mother of James, Joanna and the other women (according to Luke's gospel). There was an earthquake and an angel appeared, which terrified the guards who ran off to report matters to the chief priests. Mary Magdalene was the first person that Jesus appeared to after his resurrection.

The women hurried back to tell the apostles what had happened and Peter and John then ran over and entered the tomb and witnessed the discarded strips of linen that had covered the body and head of Jesus.

The risen Jesus then appeared to the disciples and he ate in front of them to put them at ease, but Thomas wasn't present that day and he refused to believe. One week later Jesus appeared again and this time Thomas was present. Jesus asked him to put his finger in the holes in his hands and to put his hand into his side where the lance had entered and he said, "Stop doubting and believe." The stunned Thomas could only utter, "My Lord and my God!" Jesus then said, "Because you have seen me, you have believed; blessed are those who have not seen and yet have believed."

The Ascension: Jesus appeared to his disciples for forty days during which time he continued to teach them and he also ate with them on several occasions. Jesus was then taken up into Heaven in front of his disciples outside the town of Bethany where Martha, Mary and Lazarus lived. As they were staring up into the sky, two angels appeared and gave an assurance to them that Jesus would one day return in the same way in which he had left.

Descent of the Holy Spirit: Jesus had asked the disciples to remain in Jerusalem until they had received the gift of the Holy Spirit and so they waited in the upper room of their house behind a locked door. Ten days after the ascension the disciples were baptised by the Holy Spirit, who appeared as tongues of fire above their heads. A very powerful wind blew in the house which drew crowds of onlookers. Peter emerged and gave a speech which all in the crowd understood, despite the fact that they were from a range of different countries. He urged them to repent and to be baptised in the name of Jesus and three thousand did so that day.

The Assumption: Christian tradition has always held that Mary was assumed into Heaven, body and soul, immediately after she had died. For example the Feast of the Assumption was celebrated in Syria from as far back as the 5th century and in Jerusalem from the 6th century.

Pope Pius XII exercised papal infallibility on this teaching on the 1st of November 1950 and the 15th of August is set aside as the Feast of the Assumption. Mary was conceived without sin and lived her life without sin and so was able to be taken directly into Heaven.

The Coronation: Pope Pius XII established the 22nd of August as a feast date in the Church in 1954 but the origin of the tradition can be found in Revelation 12:1: 'A great and wondrous sign appeared in heaven: a woman clothed with the sun, with the moon under her feet and a crown of twelve stars on her head.'

The chapter goes on to describe the fall of Satan and his angels and the fight against the woman and her offspring.

Revelation 12:17: 'Then the dragon was enraged at the woman and went off to make war against the rest of her offspring – those who obey God's commandments and hold to the testimony of Jesus.'

Mary was uniquely chosen from the beginning by God to bring the Christ into our World and her special role continues as our spiritual mother in Heaven. She intercedes on our behalf to her son and tries to draw all people from sin and to his love.

Her mission of the salvation of souls is therefore diametrically opposed to that of Satan. The crown of twelve stars could represent one star for each of the twelve tribes of Israel.

The Mysteries of Light

Baptism of Jesus: Jesus was baptised at the age of thirty by his cousin John the Baptist in the river Jordan and it was John that had called the Jews to a baptism of repentance for the forgiveness of sins. As soon as Jesus came up out of the water John saw heaven being 'torn open' and the Holy Spirit descended on Jesus in the form of a dove.

The voice of God was heard saying, "You are my Son, whom I love; with you I am well pleased." It was immediately after his baptism that Jesus went into the wilderness to fast and pray for forty days to prepare himself for his public ministry and for his later passion.

Wedding at Cana: It was at this wedding that we see a beautiful interaction between Jesus and his mother Mary. The hosts had run out of wine and Mary brought this to the attention of her son. Initially Jesus said, "Dear woman, why do you involve me? My time has not yet come."

Undeterred, Mary told the attendants to do whatever Jesus asked, having full confidence that he would work a miracle. There were six massive stone jars nearby, holding in total between 450 and 690 litres of water and Jesus converted this water into the very best of wines and so this miracle is an example of transubstantiation.

It also shows how Jesus listens to the voice of his mother and this surely gives us confidence in her power as an intercessor for us. It's interesting that the Eastern Orthodox Church holds that the bridegroom at this wedding was Simon the Zealot!

Proclamation of the kingdom of God: The public ministry of Jesus with his apostles lasted for three years and he appointed 72 men to go out throughout the towns and villages ahead of him to prepare the way. He worked an astonishing array of miracles including the feeding of the five thousand and the four thousand with just a few loaves of bread and a few fish. These numbers were just men, so the figure including women and children would have been far higher!

He also raised at least three people from the dead including the son of a poor widow from the town of Nain and the twelve year old daughter of Jairus, a synagogue ruler. He worked arguably his greatest miracle, the raising of Lazarus in the town of Bethany after he'd been dead for four days. The raising of Lazarus was the final straw for the chief priests and elders who convened a meeting of the 69 strong Sanhedrin.

"Then the chief priests and the Pharisees called a meeting of the Sanhedrin. What are we accomplishing?" they asked. "Here is this man performing many miraculous signs. If we let him go on like this, everyone will believe in him, and then the Romans will come and take away both our place and our nation." (John 11:27)

From then on they plotted to take his life. The miracles should provide very strong evidence for atheists as to the divinity of Jesus and they were also described by historians from antiquity such as Josephus and Tertullian.

Josephus wrote in his work Testimonium flavianum in 93 AD:

'About this time there lived Jesus, a wise man, if indeed one ought to call him a man. For he was one who performed surprising deeds and was a teacher of such people as accept the truth gladly. He won over many Jews and many of the Greeks.'

The yoke of Jesus was light compared to the rigour of Mosaic Law and his teachings centered around true spirituality, mercy and love for fellow man, as in the parable of the Good Samaritan.

The Transfiguration: Jesus took his three trusted companions, Peter, James and John up a high mountain where he was transfigured before them and Mark wrote that his clothes became dazzlingly white and Matthew records that his face 'shone like the sun.' Moses and Elijah appeared and spoke with Jesus and the voice of God was heard to say: "This is my Son, whom I love. Listen to him!"

This was one of only three occasions in which the gospel writers wrote of God speaking. The transfiguration gave this trio a glimpse into the appearance of a heavenly body and showed how our earthly bodies will be transformed at the resurrection of the dead.

The institution of Holy Eucharist: During his ministry Jesus had referred to himself as the 'Bread of Life.'

John 6:47: "I tell you the truth, he who believes has everlasting life. I am the bread of life. Your forefathers ate the manna in the desert, yet they died. But there is the bread that comes down from heaven, which a man may eat and not die. I am the living bread that comes down from heaven. If anyone eats of this bread, he will live forever. This bread is my flesh, which I will give for the life of the world."

Then the Jews began to argue sharply among themselves, "How can this man give us his flesh to eat?"

Jesus said to them, "I tell you the truth, unless you eat the flesh of the Son of Man and drink his blood, you have no life in you. Whoever eats my flesh and drinks my blood has eternal life, and I will raise him up at the last day. For my flesh is real food and my blood is real drink. Whoever eats my flesh and drinks my blood remains in me, and I in him. Just as the living Father sent me and I live because of the Father, so the one who feeds on me will live because of me. This is the bread that came down from heaven. Your forefathers ate manna and died, but he who feeds on this bread will live forever." He said this while teaching in the synagogue in Capernaum.

Jesus waited until the night before his arrest and passion to share this meal with his disciples, as by doing this it would have the maximum effect and his words would be emblazoned in their minds forever.

Luke 22:19: And he took bread, gave thanks and broke it, and gave it to them, saying, "This is my body given for you; do this in remembrance of me."

Matthew 26:27: Then he took a cup, and when he had given thanks, he gave it to them, saying, "Drink from it, all of you. This is my blood of the covenant, which is poured out for many for the forgiveness of sins. I tell you, I will not drink from this fruit of the vine from now on until that day when I drink it anew with you in my Father's kingdom."

Jesus gave himself up as a sacrifice for our sins and so put right the relationship between God and His creation, which had been fractured through the disobedience of man. All who are baptised, and who believe that Jesus is the Son of God are a party to the new covenant that Jesus established. The covenant which Jesus created, as with all covenants, is conditional. It offers eternal life to those who have faith that Jesus is the Son of God and his sacrifice nullifies the effect of sin and renders a soul eligible for eternal life. As with all previous covenants, this new covenant between God and believers in his Son Jesus was confirmed by sacrifice and this time the sin offering was Jesus himself on the cross at Calvary.

Our Lady made her most prophetic of all appearances in the course of six visits to Lucia, Francisco and Jacinta at Fatima in 1917. Her mission was to call on mankind to repent of their sins and so to stop offending God by them and she showed a terrifying vision of Hell.

It was a mother's plea, a mother who cares for us, who asked that we turn to prayer and she called on us to make the First Five Saturday's devotion to her Immaculate Heart. She also asked that Russia be consecrated to her and said that if these requests were met, then the World would enjoy peace and many souls would be saved.

Pope John Paul II did ultimately consecrate Russia to her Immaculate Heart, but the World has turned to ever greater sinfulness and the devotion she called for has been virtually ignored.

Clearly her warning at Fatima of the global consequences of sin wasn't only for that generation! World War II was the chastisement for the sins prevalent at that time in history, so surely the offence we are causing God today is putting Mankind at risk of a far greater chastisement.

However it's never too late to heed the call of Our Lady for us as individuals and for those that do so, she has left us the most beautiful of promises.

"Look, my daughter, at my Heart, surrounded with thorns with which ungrateful men pierce me at every moment by their blasphemies and ingratitude. You can at least try to console me and say that I promise to assist at the hour of death, with the graces necessary for salvation, all those who, for five consecutive months, shall confess, receive Holy Communion, recite five decades of the Rosary, and keep me company for fifteen minutes while meditating on the fifteen mysteries of the Rosary, with the intention of making reparation to me."

Made in the USA
Middletown, DE
24 June 2017